When Time
STOPS

K. A. Russell

Edited by Jo J. Hunt

WESTBOW
PRESS
A DIVISION OF THOMAS NELSON

WestBow Press books may be ordered through booksellers or by contacting:

*WestBow Press
A Division of Thomas Nelson
1663 Liberty Drive
Bloomington, IN 47403
www.westbowpress.com
1-(866) 928-1240*

*Because of the dynamic nature of the Internet, any web addresses or links contained in
this book may have changed since publication and may no longer be valid. The views
expressed in this work are solely those of the author and do not necessarily reflect the
views of the publisher, and the publisher hereby disclaims any responsibility for them.*

*Any people depicted in stock imagery provided by Thinkstock are models,
and such images are being used for illustrative purposes only.*

Certain stock imagery © Thinkstock.

*ISBN: 978-1-4497-9607-5 (sc)
ISBN: 978-1-4497-9608-2 (hc)
ISBN: 978-1-4497-9609-9 (e)*

Library of Congress Control Number: 2013909251

Printed in the United States of America.

WestBow Press rev. date: 6/7/2013

My mother used to tell me, "Ann, you ought to write a book." Little did she know that the book would be about her.

TABLE OF CONTENTS

DEDICATION

This book is dedicated to my precious mother, Ruth Larry Isley Russell, whose courage, strength, childlike heart, and commitment to God and her family throughout her entire life left a legacy of love, faith, and hope for all of us to hold dear in our hearts forever. She fought the battle of leukemia courageously and faithfully for eight years. Not one of us understands what she experienced emotionally or mentally for a solitary moment during the final days of her life.

ACKNOWLEDGEMENTS

I extend loving gratitude to daddy, S. Lee Russell, Jr., for taking such wonderful care of mother. Daddy loved Mother throughout their fifty-nine years of marriage; in good times, poor times, sad times, happy times, and poor health in the last eight years of their lives together. Daddy was a wonderful caregiver around the clock, and a faithful husband and provider. Thank you, daddy; we lived a rich life.

Also to my brothers and their wives: Darrell and Gail, Mike and Jeni, and Jimmy and Jennifer: Thank you for your communication, love, support and always providing whatever was needed for mother and daddy while I was away on a trip. We all worked together as a family, just like we did as we grew up working in tobacco. It took all of us to see mother through her cancer. I don't know how I could have done it without you.

Thank you to Crystal, my loving daughter, for the addition of the family photographs you labored to locate and label, and the corrections and changes made after each and every edit. The completion of this book would not have been possible without your God-given assistance.

Thank you to my son-in-law, Matthew, for your eye for detail and taking the time to help us complete this book.

To Jo, my life-long friend and sister in the Lord: thank you for your tireless labor of love in the editing of grammar and the addition of scripture and colorful conversation. You were an answer to prayer.

Our sweet Aunt Carol has survived breast cancer and is living unto this day of our Lord, 2013.

I extend sincere gratitude to Pastor James Baughn for his faithfulness in weekly visits and prayer for mother during her battle with leukemia. During the finalization of this book, he was diagnosed with acute leukemia. As he courageously faces each hurdle, our family will faithfully keep him in our prayers.

Dr. Choksi, thank you for your patience, kindness and caring spirit while treating mother. She loved you very much.

A portion of any proceeds from the sale of this book will go towards the Leukemia Foundation Fund, and also the Carmelite Nuns in Ft. Worth, TX, who prayed faithfully for mother each time she entered the hospital.

IN REMEMBRANCE

Our dear Aunt Enid was diagnosed in September of 2008 with pancreatic cancer and passed away two years after mother. She fought a private and courageous battle. I can just imagine her and mother dancing and laughing together in their new bodies in that wonderful place called Heaven that Jesus promised to prepare for us. Both of them will always live in our hearts.

In My Father's house are many mansions if it were not so, I would have told you. I go to prepare a place for you. And if I go and prepare a place for you, I will come again and receive you to Myself; that where I am, there you may be also. And where I go you know, and the way you know."
(John 14:2-4 NKJV)

CHAPTER 1

The Phone Call

Isn't it strange how one phone call can turn your whole world upside down? I remember where I was and what I was doing when I received that life-changing call. It was as if time stood still, just for a moment.

It was late afternoon, and only an hour away from the end of my work day. Daddy's phone call put me on alert. He was from the old school—he never called me or my brothers while we were at work. But this particular day, I knew by the tone of his voice that something was up.

"Ann, stop by the house on your way home from work." I left immediately.

My parents were sitting in the living room, hauntingly quiet, staring into nothingness. Daddy was in his recliner, and mother in her rocking chair beside him. Mother appeared frightened—she said nothing; daddy did the talking—all of it. His voice cracked as he leaned forward softly telling the news. Mother sat there motionless in deep thought.

"A while back," he stammered . . . "the doctor ordered a special kind of blood test for your mother . . . today, he called and asked us to come by his office to discuss the results . . . Ma has leukemia."

The doctor had explained that it was not the acute type, but the slower-growing type. He did not put a time table on mother's life, but rather told them she was in remission; however, he warned that when it did attack, she would need to consult with a cancer specialist, and then she probably would begin chemotherapy.

Mother continued to sit in her silence as daddy spoke. I knew what she was thinking. She could only recall the short life span she had witnessed in her own mother, whom she had lost to the same cancerous disease years before. Her face revealed her thoughts. Daddy and I tried to console her.

"Medical technology has come a long way since you lost your mother," we chimed.

We tried to assure her that improved chemotherapy would surely help cure her, and that the advanced treatment was not available at the time her mother had suffered with cancer.

As I remember, although she appeared distraught, she still looked wonderful—I mean she did not look sick at all, nor did she act sick. The only thing that was different was that she looked very tired and confused. And daddy had begun to notice that she was easily fatigued and at times had very little energy.

A person can look perfectly well and be very sick. I learned a great deal while mother dealt with her leukemia. You cannot judge how badly a person may feel just by looking at them. I believe I went into a stage of denial, because I didn't fully understand this disease when it took my grandmother's life, and I surely didn't understand it as it stared at me in the face of my dear mother.

Daddy had also called my three brothers, Darrell, Mike, and Jimmy; they stopped by the house that same evening after work. We all sat around and chatted; all of us were in shock at the news. Little did we know what lay ahead for us as we would observe, help, nurse, and love our mother all the way through this long journey. We would eventually find it to be just as the doctor had predicted: "Tough, long, and slow."

Hindsight is truly 20/20: speaking from a daughter's perspective, I wish we had gotten the entire family together that evening, simply to spend valuable time with mother and reaffirm her that we were always going to be there for her. I now regret how we all took the news; we did our best to console mother; and then we retreated quietly from the room; we left for our homes; and afterwards, our lives went on as usual. Each of us was so wrapped up in our own emotions that we failed to do the most important thing.

I went to work the next day and cried. How was this disease going to affect my mother? What was in the future for her and our family? (*Dear God, please don't let my mother die.*)

LESSON LEARNED

When a loved one or family member receives the news of cancer of any type, plan to bring your family together over a meal, or a visit. Reassure your loved one that you are physically going to be there with them through thick and thin, along with the spiritual strength of Almighty God, Who will be there to help them get through this battle. Remind them they are not alone, and more importantly, reassure them how much they are loved and cared for.

In our ignorance, we had overlooked doing this the evening of mother's news, because our stunned minds did not allow us to understand the impact it would have on all of us. The next seven years would bring changes and challenges that we never imagined.

We learned this lesson well the second time around, when a few years later, my oldest brother was diagnosed with a type of cancer. That weekend, we brought the family together for a meal and time of gathering together, just to reassure him of our love, and that we would see him through his disease, and to try to lighten his heart and reaffirm him. Actually, this time was well spent, as it strengthened our family in our commitment to the promises we had made. God was building character in us through the trials in our family burden. This gathering not only helped him, but it helped us to be there for him in any way we could.

To my best knowledge, we overlooked doing this the evening of mother's news, out of ignorance, and not understanding the impact of such news.

My brethren, count it all joy when you fall into various trials,
knowing that the testing of your faith produces patience.
But let patience have its perfect work, that you may be perfect
and complete, lacking nothing.
(James 1:2-4 NKJV)

CHAPTER 2

Remission: A Beautiful Place

Fortunately, mother was in remission the first four years after she received her diagnosis. The most remarkable thing was to watch her continue in her day-to-day routine of living as she knew it best. She kept herself very busy over those years, enjoying the family—the children, grandchildren and great grandchildren.

Even before the news of leukemia, mother was already in the routine of having birthday lunches and dinners for everyone in the family. Each month, she would prepare huge meals and invite the entire family to her home to celebrate whoever had a birthday that month. She also called each child and grandchild on the morning of their birthday and sang to them. These were traditional things she began and enjoyed doing.

One day while I was doing some cleaning at my parent's home, I came upon a book entitled "A Mother's Journal." It was a Christmas gift given to Mother from my sister in law, Jeni. I couldn't help but glance through those pages of mother's hand-written notes. On one particular page, there was a question to the reader:

"What was done special as you grew up to celebrate your birthday?" Mother simply wrote . . . "NOTHING." *(Mother, you were a rare and beautiful, selfless soul. During your life you made up for all the things you never had!)*

During those four years, she also continued her canning and freezing of all vegetables and fruits. I can still hear her saying, "Daddy has planted enough for the entire county."

Every year she said the same thing. She usually canned at least seventy-five to one-hundred quarts of green beans alone, not to mention the tomato juice, tomatoes, and peaches. I still recall stopping by to visit one day when she and daddy were standing at the kitchen sink side by side peeling peaches for canning. I will always cherish that sweet image and loving memory.

Thank God, daddy had already retired from raising tobacco, so mother did not have to deal with that hard-working crop. She just didn't have the energy it required, but she made a special effort to visit other sick and shut-ins as well as the county neighbors nearby. She was one of the first (if not the first) on their doorstep with freshly-made ham biscuits and a pie or cake.

Many times as I would stop by the home place just to check in on them, mother would be on the phone with someone else who was shut in, encouraging them along the way. That was just the way she was—loving and selfless, always putting others before herself.

LESSON LEARNED

Don't stop living when you or someone you love hears the news of leukemia (or any cancer), but instead, really start living. Make each moment count significantly. It is not the big things, extravagant, or expensive things that mean the most, but rather, the small day to day, routine things that really matter. Make time to spend with your loved one. You will not regret it for a moment. Later in my story, you will understand why this is so important.

CHAPTER 3

Chemotherapy

Mother had been feeling unusually tired. Daddy took her back to see the doctor. Naturally, they took a blood test, and the results were not good; her white blood count had dropped down, meaning she was no longer in remission. It was time to begin her chemotherapy treatments, and it was extremely saddening, not only for mother, but for all of us. Little did we know just how much her life style (and ours) was about to change.

That day is etched in my memory, as my brothers and I sat in the waiting lobby, while daddy accompanied mother to the back room to speak with the cancer specialist. Daddy's face appeared tired.

"It's time to begin ma's treatments . . . Doc said he couldn't cure ma's disease, but he could prolong her life with the chemo."

Daddy took mother to her first and most all of the treatments. As a flight attendant, I was at work on some of the days and unable to join them, though my heart was always with them. Anytime Daddy or I could not take her to the treatments, my sister in law, Gail, would gladly jump in, pick mom up, and save the day.

I saved the voicemail from mother letting me know that she and daddy were back from getting the first round. Her voice sounded frail, "It took an hour to pump the stuff into my veins."

She received all of her chemo intravenously. My heart would always feel sad and sick, because I wasn't able to be there with her until I completed my trips.

When I arrived home from a trip, I purposely didn't go directly home. My first stop was to visit with mother. As always, she was eager for any of the children to stop by and spend time with her. She loved our visits.

The first round of treatments began with one per week for six weeks. With each treatment, mother got weaker and a little slower. The first treatments took an hour. After her completion of the first six weeks, she was allowed to go home for a few weeks, while following up with her doctor every four weeks. It was an exciting moment to receive news that the chemo treatments were taking effect, and putting mother back into remission once again. With this good news, she could stop the chemo, and begin to live as usual once more.

We could always tell when Mother was having a good day! She would be up and about in the kitchen, humming and doing her usual three meals a day for daddy, and taking care of household chores. It was a beautiful sight to behold, after seeing her so sick from the treatments.

LESSON LEARNED

Do not allow your loved one to be alone during treatments! I cannot stress the importance of this enough. When chemotherapy begins, try to arrange your schedule (or someone else's in the family) to go with them to every treatment. If possible, sit with them while they receive the treatments, just to keep them company, and remind them they are not alone during this scary chapter of their life. Stay close. Hold their hand, read to them, reminisce about the good ole' days, etc.—minimize the stress.

This is My commandment, that you love one another as I have loved you. (John 15:12 NKJ) Be kindly affectionate to one another with brotherly love, in honor giving preference to one another.
(Romans 12:10 NKJ)

CHAPTER 4

The Hospital

Sometimes out of the blue, mother would get a high temperature, feel really ill, or suddenly catch a cold. Any of these conditions would send her to the hospital, only to find out that she had pneumonia. As I mentioned earlier, mother feared pneumonia, because her mother suffered with the same disease, but it was pneumonia that actually took her life.

When mother had her episodes of pneumonia, it was an emotional roller coaster for her and the entire family—we had no idea what the outcome would be. Daddy, my brothers and I decided very quickly that we did not want our mother to spend even one night alone at the hospital. One never knows what could happen. All four of us took turns staying overnight with her every time she was hospitalized. We sent daddy home each night, so he could get his rest and look after the farm.

These were precious moments that would be cherished forever. Sometimes mother was unable to rest during the wee hours of the early morning, around 2:00 a.m., and we would just sit quietly in the hospital room reminiscing about our childhood days growing up on the farm. Sometimes she would share stories of her childhood. Although it was difficult to get any rest or much-needed sleep overnight in a hospital room, it was a special gift for us to have this time with her. We had the peace of mind that one of us was "on watch" in the event of an emergency, and now that we look back, all of us are so grateful to have shared those hospital stays with her.

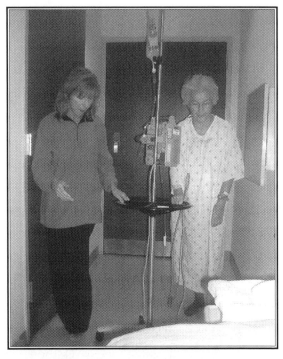

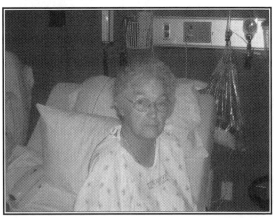

Have you ever spent the night in one of those recliner chairs in the hospital? God bless you if you have. Please do not expect a good night's sleep if you have to stay over. Sometimes I wonder if they purposely supply those chairs so visitors will reconsider and leave! Sounds of the blood pressure pumps, and the beeps of the various machines in the room will surely keep you awake. If that isn't enough, the noise from carts banging, phones ringing at the nurse stations will finish you off. Just before daybreak it seems to get a little quieter . . . aah . . . finally, you might dose off. Abruptly at 6:00 a.m. breakfast . . . it begins all over again . . . get the picture? I smile as I write this . . . despite the awful chairs and the various noises, it was well worth the lack of rest to be with my mother while she was confined in the hospital.

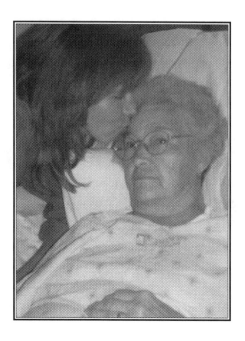

I have no regrets about those precious times we spent together. She did not always feel well, but we made sure she was never left alone. There was always a family member with her who loved her dearly and who made her feel safe and secure.

LESSON LEARNED

Work out a family visiting plan. This will ensure that your special sick one doesn't have to spend a single night alone in the hospital. This reassures them they are loved and cared for, and instills courage and strength in them to fight their physical illness. There is great strength in numbers. You want them to feel safe and secure, and not alone. (And, you want them to know that their sickness is not catching!)

Also, a well-devised visiting plan puts the family at ease, so have a serious conversation together. Visiting the sick harvests a two-fold blessing, and how much more a blessing when it's your Mother. What a privilege to obey the Word!

For I was hungry and you gave Me food; I was thirsty and you gave Me drink; I was a stranger and you took Me in; I was naked and you clothed Me; I was sick and you visited Me; I was in prison and you came to Me. And the King will answer and say to them, 'Assuredly, I say to you, inasmuch as you did it to one of the least of these My brethren, you did it to Me.
(Matthew 25:35-36, 40 NKJV)

CHAPTER 5

A Celebration

It was always exciting when the doctor made his visit to release mother from the hospital. I could not get her personal belongings together quick enough to get them out of that room! And mother was always just as happy as I was to get out of there—she would leave with a sense of relief—not looking back: *"I'm well enough to go home, to my family, to my own bed!"*

Mother was very gracious to everyone. She loved and trusted Dr. Choksi, her cancer specialist; she loved the hospital staff; and she loved the nurses who attended her. She was most thankful to her family who waited by her side day in and day out. But more importantly, she loved her Lord, who daily strengthened her and healed her frail body enough to allow her to return home where she so longed to be. Her face would light up with a glimmer of hope, revealing a thankful heart each time we packed up her belongings and headed home. It was a time of celebration!

Oh happy day! The family could once again visit her at their convenience, and she could look forward to eating home-cooked meals again in her favorite environment. Life was good—and more importantly, she had survived this ordeal! She had won another battle—and what an overwhelming sense of accomplishment she felt.

We would always stop by the drug store on the way home to pick up new prescriptions; then we would stop by the grocery store to pick up any goodies she had been craving during her hospitalization; then head for home. The sight of the farm in the distance would ignite a big smile on her face, and I could sense her anticipation of getting there. She had just enough strength to lift herself out of the car and onto the porch, and finally inside. It was as if she had been on a long journey, as she wandered into each room just to retouch her life, and hold it close to her heart.

LESSON LEARNED

When your loved one has been confined to a hospital room for weeks, and the day finally arrives that they are well enough to go home, take advantage of the break for yourself.

Because one of us stayed with mother each night of her hospitalization, we all were so relieved when she was able to be at home again so that we could take a rest from the exhaustive trips back and forth to the hospital.

So, when your patient is able to be at home, treat it as a special time and celebrate! Cherish those valuable days together, as each time may be the last.

CHAPTER 6

The Prayer

During this time of mother's illness, I was not happy about being away from her some times for days at a time. I could not really enjoy my work as I had in the past because of the constant, nagging pangs of guilt.

Flight attendants, who do not live near their "Base," usually have what is referred to as a "crash pad." This is a large house, containing at least six bedrooms, and (hopefully) three baths. Flight attendants share these bedrooms, usually three to four ladies per room, on bunk or single beds. This is where we spend the night before beginning a trip early the next morning or end a trip that stops after midnight, so we can fly home at daybreak the morning after completing our trip.

On one of these "crash pad" nights, I was fortunate to be bunking with one of my special Christian friends, Tameka Rand. We shared stories about our faith in Christ, childhood growing-up days as well as present every day happenings.

I know now that God placed Tameka there that night just for me. When I told her that I didn't get to spend as much time with my mother as I would like, she did something special for me. She took my hands, and she prayed an earnest prayer, out loud, and asked God to allow me to spend more time with my mother!

LESSON LEARNED

And this is the confidence that we have in him: if we ask anything according to his will, he listens to us. (I John 5:14 ISV)

The night that Tameka prayed, God heard her, and I had confidence that He would do it somehow! Later, in my story, you will see just how He answered that prayer!

CHAPTER 7

The Unexpected

During mother's remission, I was on a particular trip in Portland, Oregon. During my flying career, I learned my geography much better than I ever did in High School. In case you are not from the United States, it is located on the far western Pacific coast. In other words, Oregon is about as far from North Carolina as one can possibly be.

My alarm woke me that morning at 3:30 a.m. for a 5 a.m. "lobby time," meaning I had to be dressed, packed and ready to meet and join my crew members for our shuttle drive to the airport. After taking my shower, something strange occurred. I began to feel lightheaded, so I managed to stumble back to my bed, where I passed completely out. Sometime later, I woke up, to find myself in an unusually heavy sweat. I lay there thinking, "What is going on?" I was attempting to dry my hair, when I had to make my way to my bed again, passing out once more. I remember thinking this was strange, but the only thing I could concentrate on was that I had to get dressed and be in the lobby by 5 a.m. "I must hurry," I kept telling myself. This pattern continued for about an hour, and after passing out four times, I finally managed to get myself dressed as best I could. I don't know how, but I made it to the lobby by 5 a.m.

While waiting in the lobby of the hotel, my female airline crew member approached me, "How are you this morning?" she asked.

"Ok," I replied in an unsure tone.

Then she stopped and looking directly into my face she asked: "What on earth is wrong with you? You look sick!"

"I'll be ok, I am just thankful I made it to lobby.

"No, you are not ok . . . your skin is as white as a ghost! I insist that you tell me what has happened this morning . . . you look nothing like you did yesterday . . . tell me right now!"

That is when I shared with her the difficult problems that I had endured that morning while getting ready for work. She put her arm around my shoulder, and whispered gently in my ear, so as not to upset me with her words.

"Ann, listen to me. You need to get to a hospital as soon as possible...this is serious, and it needs to be taken care of immediately."

"How do you know that?"

"Honey, I was an RN for 20 years before becoming a flight attendant. I KNOW what I am seeing in your face. You are as weak as a kitten."

She then proceeded to call scheduling on my behalf, telling them how sick I was and that I needed to be released from the trip immediately and flown back to North Carolina, then to the ER and to notify my doctor to meet me there.

I recall speaking with my airline scheduler and she assured me that she would put me in "positive space" on the next flight straight to RDU airport. I remember my family picking me up at the airport, rushing me to the emergency room, where the doctor pronounced the diagnosis.

"Ann, you need emergency surgery now!"

She performed the procedure immediately. When I awoke, she explained to me that I had undergone major surgery, and it would require at least six-weeks of recovery time and possibly more.

Upon release from the hospital, my family and I returned to our home. Only three weeks into the six-week recovery time, something unforeseen and totally out of the blue occurred. My children and I were told to get out of our home. I was still so weak from my surgery that I had no strength to object, so we left.

Brad, Crystal and I found ourselves on the doorsteps of my parent's home at 9:30 p.m. I remember asking mother if we could stay the night. She said "yes" with open arms. The remainder of the evening, while we were still in shock, Brad and Crystal went on to explain the unfortunate events of the evening. I didn't realize it until later, but my marriage of twenty-nine plus years was over.

Sadly, a few days later, Brad and Crystal returned to our home to get some of their personal things, to find the locks had already been changed. It was no longer our home, nor ours to enter.

LESSON LEARNED

God was working things out…one day at a time. He had a plan for me and my children for the next two years.

CHAPTER 8

A Purpose

My main and most important concern was my mother's health. How was this traumatic change in my life going to affect my mother? I knew that my children and I being there all the time would cause additional stress for my parents, as if they did not already have enough! I did not want to do anything to hinder mother's outcome, or do further damage to her failing body.

I personally took Mother to her next visit to the cancer specialist. Once the doctor examined her, taking the necessary blood tests and getting her vitals, he announced the good news of remission once again! I knew the doctor should know about the new situation at home, so I explained my personal dilemma to him. I asked him if our new living arrangements could cause emotional harm to mother in her present condition. I was pleasantly surprised, and a bit perplexed at his reply:

"Your Mother needs purpose – now she has it!"

What a relief! This situation was not going to hurt my mother, but it was actually going give her a reason to live!

LESSON LEARNED

We had learned a lesson. The terminally ill need a purpose to live; a reason to carry on with their lives. This "purpose" can make such a difference--a reason to get out of bed every morning and do something meaningful.

CHAPTER 9

The Blessing

Amazingly, and with a little humor, that one night turned into two years! We spent two wonderful years with my precious mother and father with Brad and Crystal safety tucked away under the roof of a loving home. It became the greatest blessing ever bestowed upon us, for my children were allowed the opportunity of a lifetime—to watch and observe my mother and daddy on a daily basis, living and interacting with each other, facing cancer and fighting it together. They had the privilege of seeing what real love was supposed to look like—not the kind my marriage had shown them. What a privilege for my children to observe these wonderful role models.

Pride filled my heart each time I watched my children lend a helping hand to daddy on the farm, or help mother do her household chores. They would help her tidy up in the kitchen as she put hot meals on the table.

It was always wonderful for me to finish a trip and return home to my parents and my children. We would sit in the living room at night, watching TV together, snacking on mother's wonderful home cooked meals, laughing and chatting. Mother enjoyed having an orange at night before bedtime. It is a sweet memory as my daddy would peel and cut up oranges every night while we lived there; enough for all of us. I can still smell them in my memories.

Daddy would lovingly remove every little seed from tomato slices so mother could enjoy them, as she suffered from severe digestive problems when she ate seeds, nuts, or salads. And I felt fortunate that my children witnessed such a simple and thoughtful gesture.

At times, it was as if mother wasn't sick at all. I guess that may have been when denial crept into my finite mind. Daddy was mindful at all times of mother's condition, but I simply refused to believe it. She looked so good and healthy. She continued to cook three meals every day. She continued to keep up with all her children and the grandkids, including her every-day chores. But daddy knew what lay underneath all of the deceptive appearances. He knew all along that even though she looked her beautiful self, that inside her body was a raging storm. Her energy levels varied from high to low, and daddy understood that; but, I continued in denial and refused to understand. I did not want to face the fact that I was going to lose my Mother.

During the period that we lived with my parents, daddy had hip surgery. The boys and I assisted in taking care of him as well as mother. I recall one day, weeks after daddy's surgery, he was bragging about how well his hip felt, and how good his balance and legs were. We couldn't help but laugh when, without any hesitation, mother chirped, "Okay, Pa, if you are feeling that good, you can march yourself down the basement steps and get something out of the freezer for me."

Of course, daddy did just that, laughing all the way down the steps at her sense of humor! It was a grand moment!

Brad, Crystal and I look back at those two years we lived with them and, we truly realize how blessed we were to share those times with my parents together. Mother still acted like she wasn't sick at all. She always put up the best front she could manage, to do the most, and be the best she could be, all for the sake of her children and family. She just didn't want to give up or give in to that disgusting thing growing inside her body; therefore she determined in her heart to live daily with a purpose.

LESSON LEARNED

Beware of going into denial as I did, and that is my number one regret. If they do not look sick; if they do not act sick; or even if they look like they may be getting better . . . don't forget—they are sick! The naked eye can see only skin deep.

Avoid denial and face reality. Denial is not something you decide to do. It just creeps up on you because you want this person to live so much! It just happens, gradually, and subtly. Try to stay in the moment of reality. It is what it is; do not deny that something is very wrong, even if you cannot see it. Accept the fact that they are sick and leave the rest to the Heavenly Father. Continually pray for them; if God chooses to heal them, Halleluiah; if He chooses to take them, Halleluiah, they are not sick anymore. He has chosen to heal them in His way.

Have thine own way, Lord,
Have thine own way . . .
Thou art the potter, I am the clay
Mold me and make me
After thy will
While I am waiting
Yielded and still.

CHAPTER 10

Everyone Needs their Privacy

Mother was in remission and doing so well, and she also seemed to be improving! She didn't need us so much as she did two years ago, and I realized it was time to allow mother and daddy to have their home back. Now keep in mind, while we were there, Daddy was paying utilities for five adults instead of two. Of course, I helped with the grocery shopping and housework, but it still must have been hard for daddy to have three extra mouths to feed. When I think back, not ONE time did he (or mother) ever mention to me or my children of the extra money it cost them, not even once! That's just the way they were—two of a kind—always putting others before themselves.

Growing up, I always loved my Aunt Carol and Uncle Jack's home, and I was delighted to hear that it was for rent, so I jumped on it. It was not far away, and if mother needed me, I could be there in a jiffy. We moved into our new, but familiar place, and began a new life under our own roof. Yes, we all missed our daily spoiling, but at least Brad and Crystal finally had the opportunity to learn responsibility, and also keep an eye on our home while I was away on my airline trips. Also, I thought it was a good time to enjoy my kids before they left the nest. It was within that one year that Crystal became engaged and was married.

I couldn't help but notice while planning Crystal's wedding that mother's mouth broke out on the inside and out. It was difficult for her to eat, as her mouth was infected so badly. We made an appointment to have her checked out, and the doctor diagnosed her with "thrush." He gave us two prescriptions—an antibiotic for the infection and a mouth rinse to help heal the inside of her mouth. Just when things seemed back to normal we faced another hurdle.

The wedding day arrived! Mother didn't feel her best, but as always, she put up a good front. Gail was so kind to style mother's hair, and it looked even better than if she had gone to a well-known hair stylist, so she looked as beautiful as ever. I distinctly remember her and daddy arriving at the church for the wedding, and she was embarrassed about her mouth. I dug into my purse and very carefully applied lipstick, attempting to cover the blemishes. Her mouth was still sore, and she was very uncomfortable with her appearance. But she made it through and she even managed to dance just a little bit at her granddaughter's wedding!

With Leukemia in particular, anything is possible to appear, as I was slowly learning.

LESSON LEARNED

Stay as close as possible to your sick loved ones. Not everyone has the opportunity to live close to their parents, but my children and I had that opportunity, and it was such a blessing. We could get to their house in just a few minutes!

I admire friends who are able to move their parent(s) into their own homes for their last years. What a wonderful and unselfish thing to do. It stands to reason that when parents are facing their final sunset, just knowing their children are close by, or just a "stone's throw" away, gives them peace of mind. This is a priceless gift to give them—just remaining close.

Honor your father and mother"—which is
the first commandment with a promise—
(Eph. 6:2 NKJV)

CHAPTER 11

Back to the Hospital . . . Again

We couldn't help but notice that mother's condition was changing. She was getting weaker, and becoming very frail; and this time, it was really troubling. Again, we found ourselves practically living at the hospital. Tests revealed that mother was dealing with an acute case of pneumonia. She could hardly breathe, and she had developed a cough that seemed to linger on and on.

As always, my brothers and I took turns staying with mother overnight. Gail, Jeni, and Jennifer took turns taking mother's favorite foods to the hospital to stimulate her appetite, hoping for a quick recovery.

Upon my many return flights, I would always go straight to see mother during her stays in the hospital in my uniform. I just didn't and couldn't afford to waste a single minute long enough to go home and change.

This hospital stay proved to be very different from the others. One night when it was my turn to stay with mother, the nurses came in to introduce a new breathing treatment. She was to breathe through this instrument for fifteen minutes once every four to six hours as needed. In addition, they also informed us that she would be using oxygen 24/7 through a tube inserted in her nostrils.

This was a blow to both of us. I just couldn't stand the thoughts of my mother not being able to breathe on her own anymore, as she had always done. The nurse asked me to step outside the room for a short minute. She told me they could either release her that day, sending her home with the oxygen tank, or have her stay another night or two, so she could adapt to this new intervention. I opted for the latter, because it was going to affect her usual pattern of living, and possibly additional stress. The staff agreed with me. *Oh Lord, help mother through this hurdle.*

A few days later, we took mother home. An oxygen supplier came by the house. He took the empty tanks and left a supply of full tanks. It took an entire room to house the supply.

Sadly, mother was literally attached to a foreign container with every move she made. Since her and daddy's house had a long hall, I asked the supplier for a longer cord, so mother could walk around the house more freely. He agreed, and mother was able to leave her loveseat and wander down the hall and sometimes into the kitchen, just for the exercise.

Thank goodness, my job allowed me to take her to the cancer center almost every time she had an appointment. I selected the days I worked to make myself available, so daddy could tend to the farm. As always, however, when I wasn't available, one of my brothers would leave work and take mother for her treatments—as always, we all worked together.

I had been in my rental house for a year when the doctor informed me and daddy that mother's condition was getting worse. He wanted to try a new chemotherapy that claimed to slow the growth of cancer, as it was supposed to be an improvement over the original treatment. He immediately began those treatments. Each one lasted two hours each day, usually two to four days a week.

At that time, I was living alone, so I asked daddy if I could move back to live with them and help mother around the house, and assist him in taking her to her appointments. They both immediately responded, "Yes!"

I began to do more of the meals, and I kept the house as neat as possible, so mother would not have to bother with those chores. She just didn't feel up to it. In hindsight, I now wish I had let the cleaning go, and just spent more time with her.

I had lived with them about two months: I was riding down our road one afternoon and took notice of a cute house for sale by owner, just three houses away from mother and daddy's house. I loved the house, and moved quickly to purchase it. I was thrilled with my purchase, because I was so close to them that I could be there in a moment's notice of mother's emergencies. I was also happy that in my back and forth trips to work, and arriving home in the midnight hour, I would not be disturbing their much-needed rest.

I will always believe that God arranged the availability of this house for me, which was literally walking distance from mother and daddy. He shows up in wondrous ways and times—just when we need Him most!

LESSON LEARNED

When major changes occur that will alter a loved one's life style, take these suggestions into consideration. These changes may actually affect their lives forever. Not only do caregivers need to recognize the mental and emotional impact a terminal disease has on this person and the extent of any "new" stress, but they need to be responsive to the patient's "new kind of life." Try to understand that life as they once knew it will be no more! Let them know you understand what they are feeling in the deepest and most personal way possible, and assure them once again, they are not alone on their journey. You will be there until this trial has passed.

Imagine the overwhelming trauma that is circling inside their heart and mind. Be aware that Satan loves an opportunity like this; he knows that during this time of weakness, he can have a hay-day. If you feel led, pray out loud and ask the Lord to intercede and comfort them. In other words, share your concern for them with God.

Don't worry about praying a perfect prayer! God wants an honest heart, not a lot of fancy words. Humble words speak volumes to God and the Spirit will give you the words.

Likewise the Spirit also helps in our weaknesses.
For we do not know what we should pray for as we ought,
but the Spirit Himself makes intercession for us with groanings
which cannot be uttered.
(Romans 8:26 NKJV)

This is the confidence we have in approaching God:
that if we ask anything according to his will, He hears us.
(I John 5:14 NKJV)

You may ask me for anything in my name, and I will do it.
(John 14:14 NKJV)

And when you pray, do not use vain repetitions as the heathen
do. For they think that they will be heard for their many words.
(Matthew 6:7 NKJV)

CHAPTER 12

"If It Ain't Broke, Don't Fix It"

This new treatment was supposed to slow down the cancer. I was taking mother for the new chemo treatments four times every week, unless I was working. If that were the case, Gail would save the day as always. It took the entire family working together to get the job done, so that daddy would not have to take care of mother alone.

For a month or so after taking these treatments, our family began to see noticeable changes in mother's condition. Upon arriving home each day, mother would be so tired, and not her usual enthusiastic self as before. The chemo was also making her nauseated at times; the antibiotics caused all sorts of discomfort in her stomach, causing her to make many trips to the restroom around the clock, and the never-ending trips and discomfort kept her physically weak. That was easy to understand, and the family accepted her "new life style."

As mother weakened by the day, even the tiniest hint of cold weather or being around a person with a cold, she would land in the hospital with pneumonia—once again—more numerous times than I could count. Those trips to the hospital, usually a week at a time, were so hard on mother, as she would always be physically and mentally drained. The hope she once had was fading and evident by her despondent face.

I cannot begin to explain how much it hurt me to watch my mother go from her normally-well body into an "imprisoned" one that was slowly dying, and out of which she could not escape! And I could do nothing to help her get out!

Mother's constant coughing began to take its toll on her body, and naturally caused her stomach muscles to be very sore and uncomfortable.

"Lee, when do you think this cough will stop?"

"When your toes are turned up." Daddy replied.

Smiling faintly, she nodded in agreement. Her voice and her face were weary. I also noticed each time we took mother home from the hospital, that she would immediately head for the loveseat in the living room and sit down. No longer did she wander about the house, happy just to be there. Her hope was slowly diminishing right before our eyes, but I refused to recognize it. Once again, I was slipping into denial.

LESSON LEARNED

A "new" type of chemo treatment is not necessarily better than the original one. Cancer patients are at the mercy of their doctors, as well as their families. If you notice any significant changes in them, and recognize that they are not improving, but possibly getting worse, these are signals that there may be new developments. Do not ignore these signs, but rather ACT on them as quickly as possible. Speak with the patient's specialist quickly about your observations. You are with them daily; the doctor is not and cannot possibly know what is going on if someone does not alert him.

CHAPTER 13

Back to Square One

After a month or so, mother completed the round of new chemo treatments. Then the doctor once again released her, so her body could take a rest and see if the treatment had been effective. Not only was she just tired anymore, she could hardly function. She was still making exhausting trips to the restroom daily, which kept her dehydrated. So we tried to keep a large cup of water at her fingertips. We even purchased smoothies, Boost, Ensure, and anything anyone recommended to keep her afloat.

On one of her better days, she told daddy she wanted to make a pan of homemade biscuits. Daddy got all the ingredients, placed them on the kitchen table, with her wooden bowl, and walked mother into the kitchen. He sat her down at the table, and she performed her biscuit art. Believe it or not, this made her day! Daddy bragged that they were as delicious as ever! More importantly, mother was so proud that she had accomplished one of her "used-to-be" simple tasks.

Mom began waking up in the middle of the night, around 2:30 a.m., hungry.

"Ma, what do you have a taste for?" daddy asked.

"Homemade cornbread," she replied.

So daddy would patiently drag himself out of the bed, go into the kitchen and make cornbread, of course with mother's instructions. After she ate it, they both would go back to bed and fall asleep. This became a regular occurrence every night.

It finally occurred to me that I could help out by baking a pan of cornbread each day. I carefully wrapped it, so daddy could have it ready to warm without having to bake in the middle of the night.

CHAPTER 14

Dear Lord, Now What?

Mother was seated for most of the day, and she began to complain with severe pain on her bottom. This caused me to be suspicious, and I asked mother, privately, while daddy was out in the field, if I could take a look and to my surprise, she said quietly, "If you want to."

I was shocked! I could not identify what I saw. I didn't want to upset mother, so I told her she had a rash that I had never seen before, and we would have daddy take a look at it when he came in for lunch. When daddy saw the rash, he gave me a puzzled look. Neither of us knew what it was. I called the doctor's office to make an immediate appointment, explaining to them what we had found. They kindly agreed to work her in the next day.

At this point, mother was just too tired to do much talking. I explained to the doctor that since her last round of treatments, there had been many changes in her condition, but that we were doing our very best to make her as comfortable as possible. Then I asked him to take a peek at the area as humiliating as that was for her. Mother humbly obliged.

My heart sank through the floor and I cried when he announced to both of us that she had the shingles . . . I will never forget the look mother shot at me when she heard the word. She turned toward me with a heart-breaking glance, with her eyes asking, "Why?" *How much more can my mother's body stand?* Over the last few months, mother had struggled with a lingering cough, the burden of carrying an oxygen tank, the many episodes of pneumonia, the painful thrush, and now the unforgiving shingles!

It was obvious Dr. Choksi was disappointed with his diagnosis, and he displayed a humble sadness as he handed us the prescription for shingles. I made another appointment to take her back in the next few weeks, and we headed home, not talking very much. As usual, we stopped by the drugstore and picked up the medication.

When daddy heard the news, he shook his lowered head, "Um, um, um," he muttered. In order to protect mother's dignity, I asked daddy if he would do the honors of applying the salve three times a day; and of course, he did, around the clock as needed.

CHAPTER 15

The Disappointment

A month had passed since mother's last visit to the clinic. It was again time to check in with Dr. Choksi, for assessment of any improvement since the new intervention.

I recall that day like it was yesterday. While mother and I were in the waiting room after the lab had taken a new sample of her blood, we were talking with other cancer patients. One of them in particular, was telling mother that this was her "ninth visit to get her chemo treatment." Mother and I just looked at each other in amazement. You see, at this point in time, mother's trips were so numerous, that we had not given thought to exactly how MANY visits she had actually had . . . I would guess, probably in the hundreds. Although we were sorry for this dear patient, it only added to the realization of just how often mother had been getting treatment. We did not have the heart to share this news with that patient.

It was time to see the doctor. We went into our normal examining room, and waited . . . longer than usual, so I told mother I was going to step outside into the hall to check on the hold-up. As I opened the door and stepped outside the room, there the doctor stood, reading intently my mother's records and the newest reading of her blood work. You see, with cancer, it's all about the blood. It tells the true tale of what the eye cannot see, especially with Leukemia.

I witnessed with my own eyes, the doctor reading the blood tests results, along with mother's file. Upon examining her results and comparing them with the results from the past with her original chemotherapy treatment, he angrily shuffled the papers together in the folder and THREW them down on the floor at his feet. Disgusted, he placed his head and face in the palm of his hands as he leaned over his table, just staring down onto the table. I didn't understand what I was witnessing, but I felt very uncomfortable with what I had seen, so I slowly stepped back into the room with mother. Calmly, I told her he would be in shortly because he was outside the door.

When he entered the room, mother, as always, was glad to see him, because she loved and trusted him; after all, her life, her very existence, lay in his hands—she was at his mercy—and God's, of course.

With a disappointing look, he asked how she was coping with all the additional ailments. Cautiously, I asked him about the new blood results. He lowered his head; mother glanced at me with those weary eyes, "What's wrong now?" she asked.

Dr. Choksi softly explained that the new drug, which had claimed to effectively treat leukemia and improve the blood cells by killing off the bad cells, had NOT held up to its promise to be more effective than the first round of chemo treatments she had received for the first seven years since her diagnosis.

He looked at me, "Unfortunately," he explained in a disappointing tone, "this treatment has done your mother's body more damage than good."

His words explained all the upheavals that mother had been experiencing. This treatment did not uphold its proclamation—it did nothing to help my mother—her life had not been prolonged—

it had been shortened! I will never forget his final words during that visit. With his eyes lowered, his words were devastating, "Now, the cancer has returned with a vengeance."

He added that he was stopping the new chemo immediately, and he was going to begin the original treatments as soon as possible and try to counteract the harm that had been done.

Mother lowered her head in total devastation; I wept—again. My heart was broken for her. I hugged her reassuringly, "Everything is going to be alright . . . we'll just have to get you back on track with the original chemo treatments; and soon, you will back to your old self again . . . in remission . . . it's just going to take a little time." I tried to speak with assurance hoping that she would believe me. *And I so wanted to believe it too!*

As we were leaving, the nurse made an appointment for the next few days for mother's return to begin the original chemo treatments once again. We were back to square one!

In silence, we drove home. It felt like someone had just kicked me in the stomach . . . it was a painful, sickening feeling. I knew she was suffering more than I was, and that hurt me even more. As usual, she just sat in the passenger seat quietly, pondering, and struggling to take it all in. We grabbed a bite to eat and took it home, but neither of us was very hungry. We nibbled quietly.

When daddy came in from the field, I told him what had happened that day. I waited until mother went to her bedroom before I told him what I had witnessed; the reaction of the doctor, the throwing of the files in the floor!

"He should've never changed the chemo treatment that was working in the first place," Daddy cried . . . "But the doctor didn't know!" (Isn't it strange how we want to blame somebody when things go wrong?)

LESSON LEARNED

If your loved one is getting good blood results, and the treatment appears to be working, and the doctor suggests another therapy, encourage him to continue using the one that's working! But if the patient wants to try the change, it will be quickly evident whether it's working or not, because the body will begin to deteriorate as my Mother's did right before my eyes. So pay close attention and watch for the signs in such a case.

CHAPTER 16

Intense Chemotherapy

Just days after that appointment, mother began the original chemotherapy. However, unlike before, the treatments were now four consecutive days, lasting up to four hours long each day. We would arrive at 9 a.m. and hope to leave by 12 noon to 1 p.m. Mother was now receiving 590 mg Rituxan; 18 mg Mitoxantrone, aka Novantron; 45 mg Fludarabine, along with antibiotics and fluids, all of which were received intravenously.

Remember the oxygen tank? She was still connected, so we always had to lug that along to her chemo. Earlier in mother's treatments, the nurses had shown me where they kept their oxygen supply. They had instructed me to use their oxygen instead of mother's so as not to leave with a possible low tank supply. Also, the nurses had shown me where they kept their blanket warmer, so each time, I would get two or three warm blankets and place them over mother, so she would not get chilled during her treatment.

During our early-morning trips to the cancer center, we made memories together; sometimes I would stop by Biscuitville and get us a biscuit. She would save hers to enjoy while she was receiving the first medication. Occasionally, I would leave her long enough to go to the hospital café and get a bite of lunch as noon approached. Some days, if she wasn't particularly hungry for breakfast, I would stop by Panera Bread and pick up lunch and take it with us. We enjoyed our own little picnic while the medications were being injected into her then frail, little arm.

Mother knew how to crochet, and I had learned to knit and crochet while on my trips. I took needles and thread with us to those long treatments and we would sit, talk, and knit or crochet together. These memory-making routines became a way of life for both of us the following month. After that, she was allowed to take a rest from her treatments and return home for a few weeks. Time would tell if the original drugs had reversed the damage, as the doctor and our family had hoped.

It was during that time that I began working only the weekends, so I could stay with mother on week days, while my brothers were at work. We found this system worked best for everyone for the time being.

During the week, I rose early every morning, jumped into the shower, and got dressed for the day ahead at mother's house. I tried to get there as soon as possible, usually about 8 a.m. If daddy had not started breakfast, then I would. After breakfast, daddy would begin his day in the fields. I stayed with mother, prepared lunch, did the laundry, and whatever else needed to be done around the house. As I mentioned before, I wished I had spent more time with mother, and just sat with her, chatting, or enjoying a TV program. But I knew the meals needed preparing, and the house needed to be tidy, as visitors dropped by regularly to check on mother.

Usually Gail, Jeni, or Jennifer took turns bringing by the dinner meals. I would head back to my house in the evening hours, giving daddy and mother their private time together, and resting up for the day ahead.

On one of mom's better days, she came up with a bright idea! She asked me to start a "chain" of crocheting for her, long enough for a scarf. I made the chain, and she began making a scarf, then another and another. She even asked me to start the "chains" each time before I left on a trip. Upon my return, she had completed each scarf. They were beautiful!

During one of our trips to the Cancer Center, she asked me to stop by a place in downtown Burlington that was known for its embroidery. Some friends had told her about this place that could monogram initials on each scarf, one for each daughter and granddaughter in the family. Mother knew exactly what she was doing—she had a plan. Her body might have been frail and weak, but her mind was still very sound. And, more importantly, she was still thinking of others. Remember the PURPOSE? Once again, she had one!

LESSON LEARNED

If at all possible, try to stay with the patient during the entire chemo treatments, and make it as pleasant as possible. Find out what they are especially hungry for, or if they even have an appetite. If they have a hobby, or enjoy reading, join them in that hobby. Use this time to be a blessing to them and yourself!

CHAPTER 17

One Step Forward, Two Steps Backward

As we muddled along that next month, we were on edge every day as we were wondering (and hoping) that maybe the chemo treatments were having a positive effect on mother . . . that dreaded pneumonia showed up again, and she was back in the hospital. While on a trip, I received a voicemail from my older brother, Darrell. He was always good at keeping me up to date with mother's progress while I was away. I remember exactly where I was when I received the bad news, because our flight was delayed due to mechanical problems. I turned my phone on to get the message as I was standing in the front galley of the plane. I immediately called Darrell back to ask how mother was doing.

"She's okay, all things considering." He sounded unalarmed.

"Should I get off my trip and fly home?"

"Nooo, we boys have it under control . . . finish your trip . . . I'll keep you posted if there is a change," he replied in a reassuring tone.

"Okay, I'll be home in a day or two . . . plan for me to stay with her at the hospital overnight when I get there."

When I got to Burlington, I went straight to the hospital. Mother was so sick, not only from the leukemia, but from the pneumonia that had caused the nagging cough that had plagued her for so long. It was during this particular hospital stay, the doctor had told us that the ineffective chemotherapy treatments and the many bouts of pneumonia had left mother's lungs scarred. He gave us prescriptions for the cough; kept her on her oxygen; but the unforgiving cough lingered on and on.

Fortunately, we were able to take mother home, once again. Each time, she became weaker and weaker. This time, when we arrived home, she barely made it to the loveseat. And once she sat down, she only got up to hobble down the hall to the restroom or to bed. I can still see her struggling to get around with that dreadful oxygen tube in her tiny nostrils. Family members would leave for home with broken hearts.

LESSON LEARNED

Communication is essential. If you have siblings, communicate with everyone about the situation at hand. Do not hold back any information. Whoever is lending the helping hand at the time, whether it is immediate family, friends, or neighbors, keep everyone informed. It is a tremendous help for the wellbeing of the patient, and it helps keep everyone on the same page.

CHAPTER 18

She Danced

Mother's "rest" periods at home were also a rest for me. If you have ever taken a loved one to the doctor every single day of the week, for week upon weeks, then you know how taxing that can be. So, when mother had her rest periods, I felt like I was on vacation for the two or three weeks she was at home.

When the rest period was over, it was time to check in with the cancer specialist again to see if there was any progress from the last chemo.

"Okay, mom, here we go again." She would manage a weak smile. As usual, they took her blood, and we waited in the examining room for the results. The doctor informed us that things were trying to improve, but it was going to take time. He also said more treatments were needed as soon as possible to try and speed things up. He wanted us to begin those treatments immediately, just like the last time, 4 days a week for 4 weeks.

"Maybe they are working this time," mother said with a hopeful expression.

"Little lady, how are you coping with that cough?" the doctor asked.

"Ok, I reckon—sometimes I get Lee to make me a little toddy at night."

"Drink all the toddy you want—it can't hurt at this stage of the game," Dr. Choksi chuckled as he answered.

It suddenly occurred to me that day to request a copy of the blood results they were taking on each visit. In hindsight, I guess I should have requested these results long ago. But after the failure of the last chemo treatments, I wanted to see for myself how the "original" chemo treatments were improving the counts of the red and white cells. I wanted some type of documentation to show daddy and the boys just how our mother was really doing.

The nurse kindly started printing two copies each visit after that; one for their file, and one for mother and me to take home. We posted them in the kitchen, week by week, to show her progress, if any.

We still had to take the oxygen bottle along with us to every treatment, for four days a week, four hours a day, and we continued our little picnics consisting of her favorite foods, and knitting and crocheting. The nurses were all interested in my career as a flight attendant, and they were always asking me questions. I gladly shared my stories with them, and the conversations kept mother's mind OFF of herself for the time being.

Mother just HAD to improve with these treatments because it was September, and my son, Bradley, was getting married that month. Mother had promised him, while we lived under her roof, that one day she would dance at his wedding.

Thank goodness, that day came on September 23. It gave us much joy and gladness to get mother all dressed up in a beautiful evening dress, get her hair and make-up just right for the wedding and reception that evening. We have a beautiful photo of mother and daddy walking down the church isle, pulling her bottled oxygen behind them.

She had a look of pleased accomplishment because she had made it this far, with that sweet grin, with a sense of satisfaction on her face—nodding her head up and down thinking, "I made it to my grandson's wedding and will dance as I promised."

And she did indeed dance at his wedding! We have treasured photos of mother dancing with daddy, and with Bradley. Her smile radiates heaven . . . and to be honest, in thought, she probably was there.

It was quite comical to observe that evening. She would sit at the table long enough to take in a few breaths of oxygen, take the tubes out of her nostrils, and get on the dance floor for the entire night, until she was physically exhausted. It was a sight to behold for all of us. She was enjoying life at its best for the first time in a very long time, and we were so proud of her! She even did the "dose-doe" arm in arm with me—a photo I cherish.

Mother dancing with Brad
at his wedding

Mother and I doing
the "dosie-doe"

Mother and Daddy at Brad's Wedding

LESSON LEARNED

At the beginning of treatment, request a copy of all blood results. You will find it helpful to compare each reading, day to day, or week by week. Once we started receiving these results, I wish I had requested them much sooner, just for our peace of mind.

CHAPTER 19

Thanksgiving . . .
So Much to be Thankful For

We completed those four weeks of treatment and took a few weeks off. Wow, mother was glad to have them behind her, and so were we! The week following the final treatment, we once again went to the doctor to get a report. Thank the Lord; things were looking much better than before. The blood results were showing good signs, and the doctor told us to enjoy Thanksgiving.

That is exactly what mother did. She continued making scarves for the girls, getting the new ones embroidered. She was still slow moving around the house on a daily basis; she still sat on her love seat, but her demeanor displayed a little more spirit than before the treatments.

The day before Thanksgiving, she actually spent a lot of time in the kitchen, preparing dishes a day ahead so she would have them ready for the arrival of the family.

I was out of my mind with joy! To arrive at mother and daddy's the day before and find her in the kitchen was a picture I had not seen in so long; I embraced it with everything within me. How wonderful to arrive on Thanksgiving Day to see the kitchen counter filled, not only with the dishes her children had brought, but those that mother had made also! I could hardly contain myself . . . I was ecstatic!

As for mother—she wandered about the kitchen, taking in the beautiful scene. All of her grandchildren were at the kitchen table; all of her great-grandchildren were seated with their parents; and all of her children and their spouses were seated with her and daddy in the dining room. Everyone was enjoying a happy mother. What a beautiful sight!

Still not back to her usual self, she had somewhat improved over the last two to three months. More importantly, she was HERE, with us, her family. We all embraced that Thanksgiving— holding our breaths, deep down wondering if we would have any more holidays together after this one. Daddy said the grace, as always—but with his voice cracking as he prayed. This was a rich moment, not to be taken lightly or for granted. God had blessed our mother, and our family—to enjoy a Thanksgiving together as a complete family once again!

LESSON LEARNED

Make the MOST of the Holidays! Have you ever spent a holiday alone? If you have, you probably never want to again. Holidays have a way of bringing families and friends together, and those days can be very lonely without the people you care about. Whether or not the loved one has the energy, make the most of those days . . . neither they, nor you, are guaranteed the next one together—on this earth.

CHAPTER 20

The Last Christmas?

When you have spent day in and day out with a terminally ill loved one, and holidays are just around the corner, your foremost thought is, "Will they make it long enough to see this one?"

Happy day, she made it! But our nagging minds gave us no rest, and we continually wondered, "How much longer will we have her?" However, we all got busy and helped get the house decorated for mother, since she was spending lots of time on her spot on the loveseat. Everyone pitched in during the month with the decorating; one got a pretty tree; another got the decorations; another one of us made sure they were hung just right; and another did the outside decorations. We all worked together so beautifully to make things appear as they always had on every Christmas.

Mother loved Christmas shopping, but that year she didn't have the strength or energy to go shopping like she had done for years. She gave money to me and each daughter-in-law money to buy gifts for their entire family to be labeled, "From Mother and Daddy." Once we all made our purchases, we showed them to her, and then happily wrapped them for her, while she looked on with eyes of an eager child.

I remember one of my visits with mother during that particular Christmas time as being so special! We heard voices singing outside. With wide eyes, we wondered who on earth it could be! We opened the front door to find the ole' fashioned Christmas carolers from our home church, singing our most favorite, familiar carols. Needless to say, it brought great emotion and tears to daddy, mother, *and me*. It was as if angels had shown up just to bless and lift Mother up! Actually, all of us were blessed and lifted up! What a sweet Christmas memory.

The day before Christmas, once again, mother began her baking. It was much slower than at Thanksgiving, so we realized how difficult it was for her. We all baked dishes and helped fill the table with the huge feast mother was accustomed to enjoying with her family.

This Christmas was different from all others. Mother just sat there, very quietly. She was dressed in her red sweater, she looked very pretty, and her hair was nicely styled. Although she didn't lose her hair, it was much thinner than it had been from the chemo treatments. But Gail had cut and trimmed it into a very becoming style, and it looked very neat. She was seated in her usual spot as all the children gathered in the living room before the meal, for the traditional reading of the Birth of Jesus Christ from the Bible, as daddy had done all of our lives.

All our eyes were on mother. She bowed her head as daddy's voice cracked in the reading of the scripture. I keep that photo of her handy in my room, because I love her expression of humility so much.

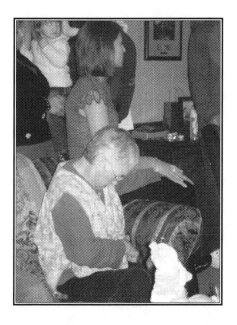

Oh how I wish that all of us could have said something memorable that evening about our mother, to reassure her of our adoration. But we did not. (Why didn't someone think of that?) We just sat and stood quietly, taking in the moment. All of us were thinking, "Is THIS the LAST Christmas we will have with our mother?" I wanted to say something loving, to honor her life, but I knew if I even opened my mouth to speak, I would cry; it was just too emotional at that moment to speak. Deep down, I wondered if she knew what we were thinking. None of us wanted mother to suspect that we might be thinking *that*, so all of us just kept quiet.

But as I recall, mother spoke a few words—very few. She simply said she loved all of us, and that she was grateful the Lord had allowed her one more Christmas with her much cherished family. (So, she *was* thinking the same thing that we were thinking—is this going to be my last Christmas with them?) It brought tears to everyone's eyes. I truly do not know if our being quiet was the proper thing to do or not. But that was the way it took place. We all gave thanks that the family was together and how blessed we were that mother and daddy were there with us to share the holiday.

Someone said the "blessing," I believe it was Darrell. Then the kids rushed into the kitchen to start piling their plates with the feast mother had prepared, and once again, we ate at the large dining room table; mother, daddy, and their children, with the grandchildren at the kitchen table once again, just like we did at Thanksgiving.

It was time to distribute the gifts that had been placed under the beautiful Christmas tree. Mother always enjoyed watching each and every one receive and open their gift from her and daddy. It always gave her much more joy to give than to receive. She loved the anticipation of everyone's reaction.

But this Christmas, we asked mother to take a seat at the dining room table where we placed all of her gifts. She was overwhelmed with tears and eyes of disbelief. We have photos of such joy and wonderment. On this particular Christmas, my close friend, David Test, was present to share Christmas with our family. David took pictures of everyone's family, as well as a photo of our family with mother and daddy. These photos are priceless. Mother and daddy are laughing in most of them. She was just so filled with joy that particular Christmas Day. It was like she was trying to savor the event, as if she already perceived it to be her last.

(From Left—Jimmy, myself, Michael, Mother, Daddy and Darrell)

Darrell & Gail with their sons and daughters-in-law,
Travis and Erika (Left), Brandon and Erin (Center) with
granddaughters Mackenzie & Erianne

*Bradley & Lesha (left), Crystal & Matthew (Center),
myself with David Test*

Michael & Jeni with their kids, Scott and Jennifer

*Jimmy and Jennifer with kids, Ryan (left), Blake (middle),
and daughter and son-in-law, Tiffany and Jonathon (right).
(Tiffany was pregnant with their first child, Cohen, which was born
2 months exactly after mom passed.)*

(Each family has grown since these pictures, so my daddy has
been blessed with even more great grandchildren.)

LESSON LEARNED

During the special Holidays, take as many photographs as
possible of the loved one with family. You never know when it's the
last opportunity. And speak what is in your heart—speak! You will
regret it later if you don't say what's in your heart.

CHAPTER 21

It's As If She Isn't Sick At All

Wow! We enjoyed a wonderful Christmas with mother, and New Year's Eve was quickly approaching.

No doctors for a month! No chemo treatments! Life was GOOD. Plans had been made for the family to celebrate the present year and bring in the New Year at Jimmy and Jennifer's home. As we all worked together coordinating the food and music, we were hoping that mother would be well enough to dance with daddy one more time.

Christmas Day passed, and mother had a few days to rest in between, and she was ready for the party! Everyone joined in to celebrate all that mother had endured in the year behind her, and we eagerly looked forward to the New Year ahead for her and our family. A wonderful time was shared by all, especially mother. Once again, she danced the night away. We were thankful and a bit surprised at how well she appeared that evening! She and daddy left the party close to midnight, to get a good night's rest.

I went home, feeling on top of the world! I thought to myself, wow! "My Mother is doing great." It's as if she isn't sick anymore. Maybe the chemo has put her back into remission? Wouldn't that be a wonderful gift?

Since I had been out of work for the Christmas Holidays and New Years' Eve, I knew I needed to work a trip if possible. Since mother was doing so much better, I went back on a trip on the second of January.

Before leaving for the airport, I stopped by very early that morning, about 6 a.m., walked into mother and daddy's bedroom, and kissed mother on the forehead. She looked wonderful, and kind of sleepy. I asked how she was feeling, and she replied, "Good."

"Wonderful, I am going to work this morning, and I will be back in two or three days, ok?"

"You gotta do whatcha' gotta do—just be careful and hurry back," she whispered.

I drove to the airport, still thinking about our wonderful Christmas and New Years' together as a family. I arrived in Baltimore and began my trip. I was really on top of the world, thinking maybe mother was back into remission and the worst was behind us.

Little did I know what was going to happen next. I worked the first day of the trip, called home, and everything was fine.

On the second day of my trip, I received a phone call from Darrell. "We dropped by to check on mom . . . her breathing wasn't normal, even with the additional oxygen, so Gail and I rushed her to the ER. The doctor decided to keep her hospitalized—for days."

I told Darrell I would stop my trip and head home. He assured me there was nothing I could do and for me to complete my trip, then return home and to go straight to the hospital.

I was a nervous wreck. It was difficult to concentrate on my work and my duties. I couldn't think and I was confused. How could she look so good? How could she dance and breathe so normally, and then end up back in the hospital? I just couldn't understand this. *"Dear God, please help me get through this trip."*

LESSON LEARNED

Sometimes, things are not as they appear. Keep that in mind . . . changes can occur quickly, as I have mentioned in an earlier chapter. A terminally ill patient can literally dance and die in the same time frame.

CHAPTER 22

This Cannot Be Real

I arrived home and drove straight to the hospital. There was a "rattling noise" when she breathed. This was Greek to me. What did it mean? I soon found out. When a person is close to expiring, they may get the death rattle, even with the use of oxygen.

Mother was in the worst condition she had been in over the course of the past seven to eight years. She actually came very close to expiring. But it was not yet her time. In a few days, she was released from the hospital.

It was January 1, and I was on a trip. Around 9 p.m., Darrell and Gail had been out and about, and decided to stop by to check on mother and daddy. He later told me that he and Gail walked into the living room where they were seated, and they both noticed that her breathing wasn't normal. He asked daddy how long she had been breathing like that—daddy's hearing wasn't the best, and he had not even heard it! They immediately knew what was happening, and drove her to the ER.

While waiting with mother to get her admitted, a nurse came over and asked mother if she had a living will. She looked at Darrell for the answer. Darrell lovingly responded. "Mom, you have to make that decision, I can't."

Then the nurse asked mom about a natural death, or machines, food and water. Once again, she looked to Darrell for the answer. "Mom, you decide; it's your life and your decision." After that, she was admitted to the hospital. That evening, they stayed with mother overnight.

The following night, I was still on a trip, unaware of what was happening at home. All Darrell had said to me during our phone conversation was, "There is nothing you can do." I didn't read anything into his comment and was not aware that she was so close to death.

Mike and Jeni stayed with mother the following night at the hospital. Jeni described it as, "We just held our breath each time your mother took one . . . she would breathe in, wait a moment, and finally breathe out . . . neither of us slept a wink that night because the rattling that was coming from congestion in her lungs was so disturbing. After a little coaxing, she mustered enough strength to give us a big cough, producing a large mass of infection . . . after that, her breathing improved a bit for the remainder of the night."

They noticed a bracelet on mother's wrist that was not there before her admittance. It had the initials "DNR," which means "Do Not Resuscitate." This troubled us greatly; after all, we wanted the staff to assist mother in any way possible if something happened to her.

Later that evening, when Darrell and Gail came to visit, Mike explained the conversation between mother and the attending nurse the night before. Mother had told them, *"Just let me go."*

By the third day, I had completed my trip, and headed straight to the hospital. I had NO idea of the condition in which I would find mother. I just couldn't believe what I saw when I stepped into that hospital room—my mother lying there, weaker than we had ever witnessed in the last few years. I was in shock. How could this be? The night before my trip, she was feeling pretty good! How could she go backward so fast? Since I had been gone for three days, I wanted to stay with her that night.

While mother was resting, appearing to be asleep, a nurse came in the room to check on her, around 2:30 a.m. She noticed I was awake. I told her I couldn't sleep, just thinking about how close we came to loosing mother. I was shocked at the nurse's question.

"Would you like for a Chaplain to come in and talk with you?"

"No," I replied emphatically.

"Well, would you want to leave the room and go to the chapel and meet with a Chaplain?" she asked me again.

"No, I am not leaving my mother alone." I was irritated.

"We've seen this situation before, and we have all agreed that your mother will not leave the hospital this time, alive. The doctors have said that she has the death rattle, and no one has ever survived it," she answered, "so you need to get yourself prepared!"

A few minutes later, she asked me again if I had changed my mind.

"No, I want time alone so I can talk to God. He is the One who is in charge, not the nurses, and not the doctors. And He is going to get her well enough to go home," I replied.

"Call me when you've changed your mind," she spoke as she left the room.

Once the nurse was out of the room, I cried as silently as I could, so as not to wake mother. I cried out to God. Then, I heard a still soft voice: "I am GOD, not the nurse. I will decide when it is time to bring your mother to me."

I told my Heavenly Father I just couldn't let her go just yet. I had not ever lived life without mother, and I wasn't prepared. I asked Him to give her the strength to go home one more time. I told Him I knew He was in control and no one else. I also asked Him to show me how to help mother.

Then I walked over to mother's bed, leaned over her, and whispered, "Mother, can you hear me?"

She nodded her head, "Yes."

"Did you hear what the nurse said?"

"Yes," she replied softly.

That's when I got upset to say the least!

"Mother, don't pay any attention to what the nurse said—she "ain't" God . . . He's the only one who knows when He wants you to go to Him . . . no nurse . . . no doctor. And you're not leaving us until He is ready to take you. Do you understand me?" She opened her eyes, looked at me, and smiled.

"Get well so you can get out of here and we will take you home again; and I will take care of you the best I can, along with the boys and daddy. Do you hear me?"

She smiled even bigger, and replied, "Ok—I'll do my best."

After our conversation, I told her how much we admired her for her courage to fight so bravely. But, this "rattle attack" had taken its toll, and I could tell she was giving up.

I learned later from Mike that actually, on day two of that hospital stay, the doctor had noticed a slight bit of improvement in mother's condition, and had told her that she could go home in a few days, if she could improve enough to walk with the walker down the hall and back. Obviously, the nurse did not know about this communication.

Be still, and know that I am God; I will be exalted
among the nations, I will be exalted in the earth!
(Psalm 46:10 NKJV)

LESSON LEARNED

No one on this earth knows the hour or the time. Only our Heavenly Father . . . Don't let a single person, a nurse, or a doctor, try to tell you when the time has come. Remember WHO is in control!

Know that the LORD, He is God;
It is He who has made us, and not we ourselves
We are His people and the sheep of His pasture.
(Psalm 100:3 NKJV)

CHAPTER 23

The Challenge

"You have a new great grandbaby due in only a month," I reminded her . . . surely you want to be here to witness that birth . . . and your fifty-ninth wedding anniversary is coming up in March, and you know you want to celebrate that." I was spouting anything that would inspire her to hold on a little longer, or give her a little something to hope for.

Her breathing returned to normal with the assistance of the oxygen, pumping it up to 4.5 liters, in addition to the breathing treatments, once every three hours around the clock. I knew deep within my heart that I had almost lost her during this last attack, and it was a frightening thought.

We chatted a little more before dozing off to sleep. Around 4:30 or 5:00 a.m., there was a tiny bird outside our window chirping its little heart out. Mother opened her eyes. "That little bird is surely telling us the news this morning!"

I had to chuckle. I had never heard that saying before. Coming from mother this new morning after the events of past nights was music to my ears.

Dr. Choksi came by around 6 a.m. "How do you feel this morning, little lady?"

"I'm still here," she answered. "When can I get out of the hospital and go home?"

He looked at me, and then at mother. "Whenever you build up your strength . . . try walking with your walker down the hall a couple of times; then within a few days, I will release you to go home." He continued, "Do you think you are able to manage such a challenge?"

(That was just what both of us wanted to hear!)

"I'll give it my best shot," she chimed.

I told her that our whole family would see to it that she accomplished this challenge, so we could take her home. Then the doctor told her he would check in on her later, and for her to ask the nurses if she needed something for pain or restlessness. As he stepped outside the door, I quickly followed him. In the hall, I asked, "Doctor, what do you think about this? Is she going to be ok?"

He raised his arms in the air and said, "Your mother has nine lives! She's a living miracle."

I was ecstatic! I thanked him and immediately rushed back into the room to join mother, assuring her the doctor said she would be going home in a few days.

Those days turned into weeks . . . very busy and difficult weeks. It was all we could do to get mother to eat. Her body had taken a beating with this last attack, and she had no energy and very little strength. She was in such bad condition at that time, that it was all we could do to get sips of water in her mouth.

I decided since all of us were taking turns around the clock to care for her, that I would take a notebook to her room and begin keeping track of everything. We charted her temperature around the clock, including blood pressure, oxygen, what she was able to drink or eat, potty trips, blood tests, x-rays, medications – we charted everything so we could see if there was any improvement.

I still have this book today. I can tell by each one's handwriting—which brother or sister-in-law was with mother, at what time, the date, and the occurrence. For example, Darrell had written on Jan. 4, at 11:25 p.m.:

"She had sips of water and ginger ale, and spoke a few words . . . aware of my presence, and watched TV for 16 minutes."

We all wrote detailed notes. Believe it or not, it proved to be a big help, especially in changing shifts with each other.

Jennifer, a registered nurse, was helpful. When she happened to be in the room during the doctor or nurse visits, she knew all of the appropriate questions to ask—things I would not even know to ask.

Mother had been lying in the hospital bed for so long, her lungs had filled up with fluid so much that it caused a lot of pain in her back. They started giving her morphine for the pain, in addition to antibiotics for infections.

On January 6, at 8 a.m., she actually ate eggs and a little sausage for breakfast. By 9:45 a.m., she had an enormous cough, but with encouragement, she was able to get rid of some of the culprit. We knew this would increase her chances of improvement.

At 10:00 that same morning, I bathed her and changed her bed linen. We all know the great feeling of a clean body on spanking clean sheets!

And of course, with each trip to the hospital, we all brought food from home, the bakery, her favorite restaurants—anything— hoping that she would have a taste for one of them. We knew that one key to her survival was good nutrition.

LESSON LEARNED

When a loved one has that frightening life-threatening attack, it doesn't have to be fatal just because the nurses and doctors speak it. Miracles happen every day. Never give up hope.

Also, it is such a good idea to keep around-the-clock notations by family members about the patient's diet, breathing patterns, any questions or comments they make, any changes that occur, doctor/nurses comments or questions and times these things occurred. Our family did this for mother, and it proved to be a big help for communication purposes.

CHAPTER 24

An Unbelievable Weakness

As the days passed, mother's days consisted of sleeping around the clock, waking up only for a few minutes at a time, mostly upon the arrival of her family or friends coming to see her. Then she would shut her eyes and drift back to sleep.

Her lungs were in such bad condition, the doctor said it was important to raise her up regularly, and try to get her from the bed to a chair to sit upright a few minutes each day. After a day or so, her lungs began to wheeze, and we had to continually encourage her to cough strong enough to clear her lungs. On January 7, we had to use an auto lift to set her upright in the bed, in order to get her to the chair.

On January 8, she actually stood up from her chair for two minutes before getting into bed. This was a welcomed sight after the events from the previous week. On January 9, she actually walked from the bed around to the chair, slowly and carefully.

At night time, she was receiving sleeping pills, along with the morphine for the back pain. Mike wrote that she was "restless from 2 a.m. to 5 a.m. on the morning of the January 10." She had many restless nights during this stay in the hospital. On January 11, daddy wrote that she actually walked out into the hall 20 feet. Now THAT was a great accomplishment! On January 12, daddy wrote:

"After she ate a little bit of lunch, she walked to the nurses' desk and back."

We were so encouraged each time she made the slightest accomplishment. She was still receiving her breathing treatments around the clock every 3 or 4 hours and taking many types of medication at this point. Any progress was a welcomed gift.

January 13 proved to be a very restless night for mother with much fidgeting. She finally began sleeping about 3 a.m., but the nurse came in at 4 a.m. to take her vitals. Her mouth was broken out on the inside again, so we used Duke's mouthwash to swab it out, along with her handy chap stick, which she had always kept close by.

Then on January 13, Mike wrote:

"She walked completely around the block!"

This was so exciting! She did it again on the 14th, making it her second trip around the block. Jimmy stayed with her the night of January 14, writing that she had a "good night's sleep."

Then on the morning of January 15, Jimmy wrote:

"The doctor came by and said that mother could go home tomorrow, but she will need homecare or Hospice to help her get her strength back . . . this is only Precautionary—once she improves, they will leave, after maybe a month."

That same day, she walked around the block again. Then she ate a decent lunch and had ice cream as a treat that afternoon. Darrell stayed with her the night of the 15th. Gail stopped by early that morning to check on things, and brought a bite of breakfast for Darrell and mother.

After they left, daddy and I stayed, impatiently waiting for the doctor's visit to release mother. Finally after lunch, we received the good news, and we were finally on our way home. We could sense that she wasn't herself. She just sat in the car very quietly.

When we arrived home, daddy and I assisted her while she walked with a walker up the sidewalk, lifting each leg to each step, to get onto the porch, finally getting in the front door. It was with great effort that mother was able to accomplish this task. It was heartbreaking to witness, but at least she was at home.

Then daddy and I helped her to get comfortable on her special seat. Unfortunately she was too weak this time around to make it down the hall to the bathroom, so the "porta" potty had to be placed in the living room for all to see. I felt mother's embarrassment. Once we got her situated, daddy and mother just sat there, quietly looking around. This time was noticeably different from all others, and I realized something. *I am losing my mother.*

I stepped outside of the house and went to my car, where I phoned Darrell. "Mother is not herself at all."

"Mother had gone through a lot, and it's going to be different from this point forward." He reminded me of the "death rattle" that took her to the hospital. "You need to prepare yourself, because her time here is now very limited."

I wept. "I am not ready for this."

LESSON LEARNED

If you witness the "death rattle" coming from your sick one, this is serious and life threatening. It is not to be taken lightly. It may or may not be the absolute end. We had seen God spare mother for a short time when it happened to her, despite what the nurses predicted.

If a person survives this rattle, be extremely supportive, immensely patient and caring, for the patient will need all the helpful care and support you can give them to beat the odds.

CHAPTER 25

Home at Last

It was wonderful to have mother out of the hospital and back at home. The family didn't have to drive to the hospital at appointed times to visit with her, or stay with her overnight. She got to rest and sleep in her own bed beside daddy every night as they had done for the past fifty-eight years.

However, it was very sad to witness mother's condition this time. She needed the assistance of two people to help her onto her little "portable potty." Mother was very modest, and this was humiliating for her, and it was painful for daddy and me to see her like that.

I began praying for God to give her strength enough that she could walk down the hall again to the bathroom, on her own. I told mother about my prayer, and that it would be a miracle for me to witness her walking down the hall to the restroom once more.

God honored that prayer. About a week later, she did just that! We were able to take the unsightly thing out of the living room, and mother was able to walk down the hall again! I knew I was witnessing a miracle, and I wasn't taking it for granted. She was tired from each walk, but a weak grin revealed she was glad to make it on her own again.

All of us continued on our daily notations of her meals, breathing treatments, and medications, so we would be better able to see what was needed each hour for mother to be comfortable and receive everything that was scheduled for her. And, we remained aware that at any time, God could and would say, *"This is the appointed time,"* so we gave thanksgiving to Him for every extra day we had with our mother.

Hospice nurses were visiting twice a week to check her vitals, and keep an updated record of her condition. In my desire to make sure we gave her the necessary meds around the clock as needed, I asked the nurse to fill a medication box for each day of the week, and make a list of the times to be taken. This proved to be very helpful, even for daddy.

Also, I continued baking a pan of fresh cornbread daily in the event she woke up hungry in the middle of the night as she did before the hospital stay.

I had been very fortunate in having a week's vacation from my work during her stay at the hospital, and a few days off following my vacation. Unfortunately, it was time for me to return to work. I was not looking forward to leaving mother this time.

Tears blinded my eyes through most of the drive to the airport. I had assured mother that I would be in constant contact with her along the way. I called her upon arrival at the RDU airport; then at BWI airport, where I began each trip. Then I called her right before getting on the plane to begin my night at work. If time permitted, I called in-between flights, to see how her day had progressed, and for our good-nights. I kept my phone on, as always, all the time while away in my hotel room. The only time I shut it off was during the flights while at work. If an emergency came up during the night, I was always at a phone call's reach.

Although I did a lot of crying and praying while I was away, I also used my trips as a time to rest my body. I worked hard on the plane, and slept upon arrival in my hotel rooms. This had become my lifestyle.

Once I finished a trip, I would be unable to sleep the night before returning home from pure excitement. I just couldn't wait to get there to see if there was improvement in mother's condition. My daddy and brothers were a huge help to me while I was away, always keeping me informed of any changes that may have taken place. Once again, communication was so vital.

LESSON LEARNED

A medication box filled for each day and labeled with dosing instructions is a must-have for caregivers. You can prepare one, or if Hospice is called in, they are accustomed to this request. It takes away guess work, and proves for more accuracy in dosage and frequency of the medications.

CHAPTER 26

Once an Adult, Twice a Child

It was the end of January. I arrived home from a trip and hustled over to check on mother's progress. Usually, I would find her crocheting scarves, but this time she was reading *The Purpose Driven Life*. I don't recall her reading that much as we were growing up; she just didn't have the time. During her illness, friends had given her various good books and daily devotionals, which she had begun to read. She was also watching the news and some oldie-goldies on the tube.

Pastor James Baughn usually visited mother and daddy weekly, and never did he leave without having prayer with mother. She looked forward to seeing him each week. Our family will always be thankful for his continued faithfulness to visit and pray for her.

Mother sat quietly most of the day, but she would light up when any of the children dropped by to give her a hug, visit a while, or share a meal. We figured it took too much breath to carry on conversations as she had enjoyed in the past. We continued her breathing treatments every four hours, around the clock.

Mother used to be a very early riser, always up by 6:30 or 7:00 a.m. During this time, she woke up between 8:30 and 9 a.m., which wasn't normal for her. Daddy and I were giving her about five to six tablets each morning before breakfast. I thought it was strange that she wanted to take her meds with tomato juice. It sounded disgusting to me, as I never cared for it, but it seemed to help her get the tablets all down at once.

Once we got her meds down, daddy and I would get breakfast going. He got really good at scrambling eggs for her, with a piece of bacon and buttered toast. We began fancying-up her breakfast by making different egg omelets, hoping to encourage her to eat more. It worked, and she seemed to enjoy the pampering.

Hospice continued to drop by twice a week. Thank goodness it wasn't a long visit, maybe half an hour. They mainly asked questions about her routine, appetite, and they always refilled our medicine box. I couldn't help but notice that mother's usual patterns were changing. Sometimes, she would fall asleep sitting in her loveseat. We adjusted our schedules accordingly.

At this point, I was helping mother with her baths. To minimize the risk of her falling in the tub, we placed a stool in the shower stall, and I had to help her get onto the stool. I made sure the water was the right temperature; then, I would put soap on a warm, wet wash cloth, and she would bathe as much as she could, and I would finish the job, and immediately wrap her in a nice fluffy towel so that she would not get a chill. I didn't want her to get a cold or even worse, pneumonia. Once we showered, I applied body lotion to her legs and arms so she would feel nice and smell good before I helped her into her clothes for the day. This process required all of mother's energy. At first, we did this daily; as she weakened, it became too much for her, and we went to twice a week.

I recall returning home one day from a trip. I gave Mother her shower, and while I was applying lotion on her body, she told me that while I was away, a nurse from Hospice had given her a shower.

"She told me to get into the shower myself . . . she didn't help me . . . and the water was too cool . . . and she left me sitting on the side of the bed until she went and got a towel."

The thought of my mother sitting there naked and shivering upset me . . . actually, it made me furious. What were they thinking . . . mother got pneumonia at the drop of a hat! Mother was trying to tell me, "I don't like the way the nurse does it, and would you please tell them to stop bathing me while you are away?"

I instructed Hospice never to bathe mother again. I am thankful mother trusted me to take care of her bathing needs. She used to tell me, "Once an adult; twice a child," . . . during that time, I learned what she meant.

LESSON LEARNED

When a trusted caregiver must be away from their patient for a period of time, try to arrange for someone in the family to give them the special attention they need, such as minimal baths (we used to call them pan baths), until you return. There will be times when you cannot be there every minute. But when you are there, LISTEN to their conversation, complaints, and determine what they are trying to tell you. Listen to their pleas and try to fix them! Listen with your heart, not just your ears. You will be glad you did.

CHAPTER 27

"Just Let Me Go"

During January, along with my vacation time and other days off, I was also able to give away a few of my trips, which allowed me to just be away for five or six days toward the end of the month.

But for February, I got "call duty." This means you have to be at your home base for each three-day period, whether you are called to work a trip or not. This made me sick at heart. Usually, flight attendants can give away the trips they have on schedule, but it is almost impossible to get rid of Call Duty, even if you put money on it. So I knew for the entire month of February, I would have to leave each week to fulfill my obligations at work. Of course, mother became sad when I had to leave, but she understood that I, being a single woman, had no choice but to report to work.

Mother loved my phone calls, but as she weakened, our conversations were disrupted with her constant coughing. Realizing how difficult it was for her, I made sure our calls were brief. But during February, I noticed that every time I called home, either Darrell or Gail would answer the phone for her, and bring me up to date on her condition. On one of those calls, Darrell asked mother if she wanted to speak to me. When she declined, my heart sank. *My mother is too sick to speak to me?*

"She is just too tired . . . don't think anything about it," he would always say.

"Okay . . . I'll call again tomorrow . . . maybe then she'll feel better." I spoke softly with tears beginning to well in my eyes. As I put the phone down, I broke down into sobbing. It felt like the world was crashing in on me. And somehow, something inside of me, (*that small voice again*), whispered to me that soon mother would no longer be there to answer the phone. I just knew within my heart, I was realizing the inevitable, and I didn't know quite how to handle the depth of my brokenness. I believe that was the day I accepted the fact that I was going to lose my mother.

The following day, before leaving the hotel, I called home again. This time, I spoke to daddy. Once again, she didn't have the energy to speak to me. I told daddy I would be home just as soon as I wrapped up my trip. As always, he was as comforting as he knew how to be. Daddy has that special quality—the kind that puts you at ease. He told me not to worry, that they were "taking good care of ma," and for me to concentrate on my job. That is exactly what I had to do to get through the day.

When I returned home from that trip and three-day Call of Duty, Darrell and Gail were there with mother. Darrell motioned me to follow him to the kitchen, where mother could not hear us.

"Ann, there is something you need to know . . . while mother was in the hospital, a nurse asked her what she wanted to do if her heart stopped . . . did she want them to help it beat again. Mother told her, "Just let me go.""

When Darrell told me this, I knew that mother had finally given up hope. At that point, I knew she didn't have the strength or energy to keep trying to hold on to this life, as much as she loved it and we loved her. But I sure didn't want to believe what he had told me, but for mother's sake, I had to respect her wishes.

LESSON LEARNED

It is of utmost importance to respect the wishes of the patient with cancer. When they make that certain decision, (the one we do not want to make for them) accept it, for they know what their body can endure.

CHAPTER 28

No More Chemotherapy

Once we got through February, our attention was focused on helping mother get through March for the fifty-ninth wedding anniversary for her and daddy.

I was able to work short 2-day trips for work. That meant I would leave one morning and return home the following day, spending only one day away from mother. This was important to me because her condition was changing ever so quickly. I even went by the cancer center one day to ask Dr. Choksi about Mother's next round of treatments.

"There will be no more chemo treatments," he told me shaking his head.

At the time, I did not realize the depth or the significance of his statement. Now, in hindsight, I realize, he knew he had done all he could for mother's cancer, and chemo treatments would make no difference. He knew it would be a waste of mother's energy and time to put her body through more treatments, not to mention the medical expense. I left the hospital that day in shock with the thought twirling in my head: The doctor is stopping the treatments "cold turkey."

I didn't tell mother about my visit to the doctor, but I mentioned it to daddy later. He simply shook his head and told me, "Doc knows the treatments won't help ma now." Daddy was right.

The family continued to take daily meals to mother and daddy, and dropping in around the clock to check on her condition. Jimmy bought a set of walkie-talkies for mother and daddy, so that, if daddy was out of the house at the barn, if we or mother needed him, he was just a click away. The 26th day of the month was their anniversary, and we knew mother would not have enough strength to handle a big celebration. I reminded her daily of their big day to come, hoping to motivate her to give it her all. I was confident she would want to celebrate that day with daddy. I wanted it so badly for them; I honestly believed she would force her body to hold on.

In a few days, my hopes went down the tubes. A Hospice nurse came in, took mother's blood pressure, and asked her several questions. Darrell, Gail and I were present at the time. I was standing behind the loveseat, where mother was seated.

"Mrs. Russell, if your heart stops beating, what do you want us to do?" She asked.

Without a moment's hesitation, she softy responded, "Just let me go."

I felt sick to my stomach! Darrell came over to me, guiding me into the kitchen. "You heard mama. We have to respect her wishes. She is tired," he whispered.

I could not believe she was giving up so easily! I did not want to believe what I had heard. The nurse left shortly after that conversation. I don't remember much after that. I was in a state of shock.

As each day passed, I robotically tidied the house, prepared lunch for mother and daddy, and bathed mother, if she felt up to it. By this time, I was giving her "sponge baths." As she lay on the bed, I would bathe her with a soft cloth and warm water from head to toe. Then I would help her dress, and we would walk very slowly down the hall (with her oxygen tube), and get her to the loveseat. Mother was moving ever so slowly. I refused to believe what was happening. I refused to face the inevitable. My mother was fading away, like a flower. Once again, I was entangled in denial.

LESSON LEARNED

When the physician stops chemotherapy treatments and sends Hospice, it is just a matter of time—a very brief time.

CHAPTER 29

"Don't Go"

As the middle of March arrived, I was only away from mother one night a week. I suddenly realized I should have been working two-day trips long before this month. Sometimes caregivers get so caught up in making certain their patient is taken care of, that it is difficult to remember other important details for themselves.

It was March 15, and I went by to see mother on my way to the airport. As always, I chatted with her and daddy a while, gave her a big hug, and assured her I would be back the next day. During our goodbye hug, something occurred that I will take to my grave.

"Don't go," she whispered in my ear.

It took me by surprise! I reminded her once again that I would be gone only for one night, and I would return the next day.

"Just do what you have to do," she replied with a strained look on her face.

Those words tugged at my heart. I went into the kitchen and told daddy what mother had said to me. Daddy followed me outside to the front porch, and I asked him, "Should I call work and tell them I just can't make this trip?"

"Listen here, honey," he said. "You go and do your job. You gotta' have your job long after me and your ma are gone. You take care of your work, and me and the boys will take care of ma, and we will be here when you get back."

Mother's words would not go away, and I cried all the way to the airport. That was the only time she had ever asked me not to go since she had been sick. But with daddy's firm advice, I continued on. I called home every chance I could. My brothers kept me informed of any changes in mother's condition. It was always, "Don't worry, everything is alright."

I remember that trip like it was yesterday. It was a two-day trip to Denver. On the second day, however, as we went through St. Louis, we were rerouted due to weather conditions. Scheduling ended up causing me to spend another night away from home in Orlando, instead of going back to Baltimore, and then home to Raleigh. I was devastated. I phoned daddy and explained all the rerouting problems, and that I would not be home that evening, as I had promised. He could tell from my tone of voice how concerned I was.

"Don't you worry, Ma is doing the same. You do your job, and we'll take care of Ma."

We arrived in Orlando late, and it was midnight before I actually got to the hotel. I was mentally exhausted. I set my alarm on my cell phone for a wake-up call at 5 a.m. to work my flight from Orlando to Baltimore.

At 4:00 a.m., my cell phone rang. I jumped from my bed thinking it was the alarm, only to find that Scheduling was calling me, with the message that I was being rerouted again the next day because they needed me to work a flight to Chicago. For the first time in my career, I asked them if they could find someone else to work the flight explaining, "All I want to do is get home to my sick mother." The scheduler replied, "No, we really need you to work this flight."

In all my years of working, I never argued with authority. I agreed, hung up the phone, and went to the airport as scheduled the next day. Upon arrival at the Orlando airport, I learned my flight was again delayed for three more hours. This meant there was no way I was going to make it home again that night. I had this urgent feeling inside that I needed to get home quickly. I went to the employee office at the Orlando airport and spoke with a supervisor. I explained my situation to her, and she was very understanding. She worked it out for me by rearranging my schedule so that I would not have to go to Baltimore before going home. This lady must have been my angel for the day, and I will always be grateful to her for her insight and empathy.

I called daddy and told him I would be home as soon as possible. This time he said, "Gooood."

Once I landed at the Chicago airport, I immediately went to the gate and took my seat on that flight. I arrived into Raleigh that night at 11 p.m.; I drove straight to mother and daddy's at midnight, and used my key to get in the front door, and tippy-toed quietly down the hall and into their bedroom. I gently kissed mother on the forehead.

She whispered, "Good. You are finally here." I apologized for my delay, told her to get some good sleep, and that I would see her the next morning. "Now everything will be alright," she said, and she went back to sleep.

I went home and fell into my bed exhausted. I was so thankful to be home once again. I fell asleep thinking about the events of the past few days, but mostly about what mother had whispered to me.

During that time at home, my brothers told me that before mother had taken a turn for the worse, she actually had walked around in the yard for a while, admiring her flowers, gazing at the trees, speaking to the dogs, and just taking in everything outside.

"She even helped me a little in the greenhouse, planting things," Daddy added with a twinkle in his eye.

It had been a while since I had seen daddy smile.

LESSON LEARNED

When a patient says something out of the ordinary, pay attention, and if possible take time to ponder what they tell you. How I wished a thousand times I had listened to mother when she simply said, *"Don't go."*

CHAPTER 30

She Chuckled

The following morning was Sunday. I jumped out of bed as usual, got showered, and went down to mother and daddy's house. Much to my surprise, mother was still in bed. It was 9 a.m., and daddy was preparing for Sunday School, where he had taught the men's class for as long as I could remember.

But this morning, as I sat mother up in her bed, and told her how happy I was to be home again from a trip, she said, "I would rather daddy not go to Sunday School or church today." I continued to help her dress, and laid her down on her bed while I went to the kitchen to get her meds and tell daddy what mother had said. Without any questions, daddy stayed home that Sunday morning. He and I both went back to the bedroom to sit mother up and give her the required meds with her tomato juice. As we were together taking care of mother, I commented, "Isn't it interesting that mother has taken a liking to cornbread?"

"No," daddy replied. "It isn't unusual at all. Ma knows cornbread is a good life sustainer."

I recall saying in a slang, "Well, who woulda thunk it?"

At my comment, mother chuckled! I said, "Mother! It's so good to hear you laugh . . . what do you find so funny?"

She replied, "Thunk it?"

Daddy and I grinned as we were getting her meds in her . . . we had not heard her laugh since New Year's Eve!

I stayed with her and helped her get into her clothes while daddy went back into the living room. Once mother was dressed, I walked her down the hall and helped her onto her loveseat. I asked her what she would like for breakfast. She said she wasn't that hungry, but daddy and I prepared eggs and toast anyway. She only ate a small portion and said she just wanted to sit and rest.

The three of us spent the Sunday morning watching Dr. Charles Stanley and just talking. Darrell and Gail were preparing lunch and bringing it over, so thankfully, I didn't have that to do. After church, they came in with our lunch. I will never forget that meal.

Darrell and Gail sat with daddy at the kitchen table to eat, and I took a plate to mother, and sat down with her. We sat together, across a small TV tray, while we ate our lunch. I told her to pretend we were having a little tea party together. She smiled. However, I noticed mother wasn't hungry at all. She hardly ate anything. What little she did eat, I fed to her, and this was strange.

"I'm just not very hungry," she said in a voice that sounded like a child.

I attempted to put another spoonful of food into her mouth, which she refused. I gave up and took our plates back into the kitchen. I showed mother's almost-full plate to Darrell, and began washing the dishes.

"Sis, you know, mama won't last long without eating."

"I know it." Immediately, I slipped right back into denial. I did not want to think about it, and I certainly didn't want to hear those words.

That afternoon, all the boys and their wives came by to visit a bit with mother and daddy. But I also noticed something else strangely different from other visits. As each brother came in, mother immediately raised her arms to embrace them, one by one. She had not had the strength to raise her arms, even for me to give her a sponge bath, so this really caught my attention. I went over to her, and said, "Mother, I see you are handing out hugs today, may I have one too?" She raised her arms and embraced me as well . . . little did I know the significance of that embrace.

LESSON LEARNED

Cherish each chuckle and hug, for you never know when it will be the last. And if the patient suddenly stops eating, take note—their body is rejecting food for a reason.

CHAPTER 31

March 19 – A Horrifying Morning

The boys and I visited with mother and daddy most of that Sunday afternoon. Then we left for a while to give them a break; I went home to catch up few things around the house, since I had been away.

I returned around 7 p.m. to check in on them, and everything seemed to be the same. I stayed a little while, then returned home to get some rest, and went to bed around 10 p.m.

At 10:30 p.m., my cell phone paged me with a text message from Darrell. I scrambled out of bed, half asleep, threw on some clothes, and immediately drove back to find all three boys sitting in the living room talking with daddy.

Apparently, a short time after we all left, daddy noticed mother was having trouble breathing. We decided that someone needed to spend the night there, so I volunteered. I set my alarm for 3:00 a.m. to give mother her breathing treatment, which would help her rest more comfortably. I went into the middle bedroom and prepared the bed for daddy because we had mother propped up on several pillows in their bed, and daddy couldn't sleep on those pillows.

I fondly remember daddy going into their bedroom and talking softly to her and kissing her goodnight. Then I made sure daddy was comfortable in his bed. I went in to tell mother good night, kissing her forehead. "Mother, I'm in the next bedroom, and if you need anything, please let me know." She replied with a little nod.

Finally, all three of us were in bed for the night. I lay in that bedroom, just across the hall from mother, thinking about what might be in store for the next day. I tried to pray myself to sleep; I was so exhausted, that I could not go to sleep, so I watched the clock until 3 a.m.

I went in to check on mother and give her the breathing treatment. She was still propped up on the pillows, but she was very sluggish. I told her I was going to give her a breathing treatment, and I placed it on her nose and held it for her. She just lay there, breathing. When it was completed, I kissed her once again on the forehead; told her I loved her; and that I was going to go home and get in my bed for the rest of the night. She was still sluggish, and I didn't want to disturb her rest, so I left. By then it was around 3:30 a.m. I knew Michael was going to drop by at 5:30 a.m. for the next breathing treatment.

I went home, crawled into bed, and slept until my cell phone chime woke me. It was a text message from Michael asking me if I gave mother her breathing treatment at 3 a.m. I knew he was with her, so I called him back.

"Was mother coherent when you gave her the breathing treatment at 3 a.m.?" he asked.

"Yes, she was . . . what's wrong," I asked.

"She is not responding . . . hurry!"

I jumped out of bed, dressed quickly, and immediately went back to the house. Michael and Jennifer were in mother's bedroom. They were struggling to pull her back onto the pillows.

"How did she get down there . . . she was on the pillows when I gave her the breathing treatment," I told them.

We all tried to get her to speak to us, but she did not respond. She didn't budge. *What is happening in front of our eyes?* We continued trying to get her to speak, to open her eyes, but there was no response.

"Michael, has anyone called Hospice?"

"No," he replied.

I called Hospice and explained the situation. I was told they would send a nurse as soon as they could. It must have been around 6:30 a.m. Hours went by and Hospice had not arrived. We were all wondering, "What's going on...we called hours ago."

Mother was still not responding, and we began calling everyone in the family to let them know. It was chaotic – and, where was daddy?

He had not been involved in the commotion: he just sat in his recliner, very calm and quiet. Daddy was not wondering why Hospice had not rushed to the house. He knew why—mother had signed a DNR! Remember, she had told them, "Just let me go."

LESSON LEARNED

When the patient does not respond in any way, to your voice, to movement—it may be the appointed time! If they have signed a DNR, do not expect Hospice to arrive quickly, as we did.

CHAPTER 32

This Cannot Be Happening

I was in a fog. I called Brad and Crystal. They both got off their jobs, and arrived soon with their spouses, Matthew and Lesha. At the same time, my brothers were calling their children, to alert them about mother's condition; Jennifer called Aunt Enid in Florida. Gail called Carol and Billy in Burlington. Aunt Enid and her family caught a flight the very next day to North Carolina.

Sometime that morning, Jennifer and I were discussing mother's condition, and trying to figure out what we could do to get her to talk to us, or just open her eyes. But nothing we did was successful. We both decided to run home long enough to get showered, because we thought we might have to take her to the hospital again. I was only gone 30 minutes, long enough to get clean. I remember I didn't dry my hair or put on make-up because I felt very uncomfortable being away from mother, even for a moment.

Throughout mother's illness, my close friend, David, would call his mother because she contacted the Carmelite Nuns each time mother went into the hospital, asking them to pray for mother. David called me at 8 a.m. I remember that phone call like no other. We had not talked to each other for several weeks. I asked him why he was calling that morning. He said something inside him told him he needed to call. That's when I burst into tears and told him mother was not responding to anyone or anything. I asked him to please get his mother to contact those Nuns again! Get help, please! He assured me he would contact his mother, call back in a little while to check on my mother, and catch the first flight in the morning.

I believe Hospice finally showed up around 9 a.m. But this time it was very different from all other times. They usually sent one nurse to visit mother and take her vital signs. This morning, there were THREE ladies. I was gently rubbing mother's forehead and talking to her when the three ladies approached mother's bedroom. I also recall saying, "This can't be good—why are there three of them?" I wasn't feeling good about this at all.

I had to leave mother's side so they could check her, so I went into mother and daddy's bathroom, and guess what I started doing? Cleaning out and straightening up the darn closet . . . of all things? I didn't want to be far from mother, and I had to DO something to keep myself busy, so I cleaned out the closet? To this day, I wonder what in the world was going through my feeble mind to do such a thing.

Then one of the nurses called me aside and took me into the living room, where she proceeded to tell me to prepare myself for the worst. She told me when people are not responsive, they were in the process of letting go of this world. I immediately told her exactly what I thought. I told her only GOD was responsible for life and death, and she would only go when HE decided it was her time. In other words, I was not at all interested in anything this lady was trying to convey to me. I just couldn't let go of mother.

I recall after leaving the company of that lady, I walked down the hall, glancing into mother and daddy's bathroom. I happened to see our daddy. He was standing in front of their bathroom window, looking out. He just stood there. I thought to myself,

"What is going through daddy's mind right now?" It was a sad sight. I stopped and watched him for a moment. He never turned around to see me observing him. That picture will forever live in my memory.

I then stepped back into mother's bedroom where all three boys had gathered. They were all standing around mother, along with the nurses. Mother's brother, Billy, was standing at the foot of her bed, trying to coerce mother into talking. Nothing helped, though. Mother was still not responding. The nurses told us they had given her medication to make her comfortable. I didn't know what that meant at the time. But now I see more clearly.

Then the head nurse turned around, looked straight at me, and then she actually POINTED her finger at me. I froze. She told me, "Your mother is waiting for YOUR permission to go." At that, I turned around, ran down the hall, right out the front door of the house. I ran as fast and as far away as I could, crying my heart out. I ran out behind the cow barn, and fell to my knees on the grass in front of mother's bed of irises. That was when I had my battle with God Almighty, and I began my wailing.

I am here to tell you that what you see in the movies when someone loses a person they love so much…how scenes fly by in their minds of wonderful memories during their lives together, is really true! I was begging God not to take my precious mother, and as I was begging, pictures of my childhood flashed before my eyes in my mind…all of them with my mother by my side. The scenes began when I was a little girl, and they ended that day, as I humbly knelt in the grass in front of mother's irises. I didn't know a human heart could hurt that badly and survive the agonizing pain.

Then Crystal and her husband, Matthew, showed up. "What in the world is wrong, Mother . . . Mawmaw is tired, and she just can't keep on going like this . . . you know she will be out of her misery when she lays her eyes on Jesus . . . I understand how difficult it is for you to give her up, but this is best for Mawmaw."

I remember asking God to forgive me if I appeared to be disobedient to His will and selfish not to let go of mother. They helped me back to my feet, and we all walked back into the house.

What lay before me was going to be the most difficult moment of my entire lifetime. There was no choice in the matter. Nothing between heaven and earth could change the mind of God Almighty. As my daddy said, "There is nothing on the face of this earth anyone can do at a moment such as this."

LESSON LEARNED

When a loved one becomes non-responsive, stay as close to them as possible, even if medical staff are present. If you are at home, do not do as I did and make yourself "busy" . . . and then run away from the inevitable. How I regret the mistakes and choices I made on that last morning.

CHAPTER 33

Speak From Your Heart & Soul

Once we got back into the house, I immediately walked down the hall into mother's bedroom. The nurses and boys were still there, standing around the bed. Without reservation, I told them I needed a moment with mother. At my words, everyone left the room, without any questions.

I gently kissed mother's forehead, held her hand, and whispered into her ear as she lay there. Her eyes were shut. All I heard was the sound of her breathing, very normally. All was quiet.

I told her many things that were dear to my heart, and only for mother to hear. Little did I know that this was going to be the last time I would or could share with mother those things near to my heart and soul. I was so fortunate to have this brief moment alone with her. I told her daddy loved her dearly, and it hurt him to see her suffer, and he didn't want her to go.

All was normal.

Then, I couldn't help myself. I broke down, crying. I told her I didn't know how I could live without her. I told her I knew she had to go, but we were going to miss her soooo much. I couldn't stop crying.

Then something significant happened.

The breathing was not normal anymore. She would take a breath in—wait a moment—and then let it out. It happened immediately after I told her how much we would miss her. She HEARD everything I had spoken to her. She understood everything I had said. A voice inside me said, "Pay attention to what you see happening." I stopped whispering, and noticed again, the breathing changed. Then, that same quiet voice spoke again "Go get daddy—fast! Mother will want him here." I hated to leave her a split second now. But I ran down the hall to get daddy, and met Darrell. I said. "Get daddy—quick! Mother's breathing has changed."

Daddy had not expected this so soon, "What?" he asked, "now, this quick?"

Pastor Baughn, who had faithfully visited mother weekly, was there, along with mother's family; all her children and their spouses; a few grandchildren and their spouses, along with two of her siblings, her sister Carol, and her brother, Billy.

We all surrounded mother; daddy was holding mother's hand, the preacher holding their hands. Darrell, Mike and Jimmy all stood on the other side of the bed, holding her other hand. I remember getting on my knees at the foot of her bed at her feet. I remember how totally humbled I felt that moment to feel the presence of the Creator of life, the Creator of the entire universe. I knew HE was in the room with us at that very moment. To know HE was the first thing mother was going to see when her soul left this earth, her weak and frail body to be left behind until That Day of Resurrection! To know HE gave her life, and only HE alone had the right to call her home to be with HIM.

We all held her close at heart, as we watched her slip away from this life into the next. She drifted softly, tenderly, and peacefully, within seconds. Once her spirit left her body, we knew her body was just that—a body that once held her beautiful spirit.

This was by far the most humbling experience in all of my life. It was a time filled with great, agonizing sorrow and pain in letting go of that dear loved one—a pain so intense I wondered if I could even survive the agony—to an awesome peace—to realize mother was at that moment in HIS presence. She has seen Jesus face to face. She was no longer suffering.

It was just like daddy said, "You find out how small you really are, when you sit by the bedside of your loved one and watch their life pass away—and there is nothing this side of heaven you can do to change it."

Mother took her last breath on earth at 12:55 p.m. on March 19, 2007 just seven days shy of their fifty-ninth wedding anniversary. Daddy said he felt like half of him left the day he lost mother. He later shared with me and the boys the night of March 18, when he kissed her goodnight and tucked her in bed on those pillows the night before, she asked him, "Lee, are you ready for this?" He had responded. "Ready for what?" (Daddy was in denial also, but when the time came, he realized what she had meant.) The only one of us who was not in denial was our mother.

The radio next to mother's bed was softly playing. Her favorite song had become, I Can Only Imagine, which was sung by the group MercyMe.

As we all stood around her bed, and just shortly before she took her last breath, she heard her favorite song once more, just as she was passing through the gates of that heavenly place, about which we can only imagine.

There was a beautiful amaryllis in full bloom sitting in the living room that daddy had grown and given to mother a few days earlier. Later that afternoon, the same day that mother took her last breath, daddy noticed the amaryllis had dropped its bloom and withered.

The clock still sits on the mantel in their living room. Daddy said it was mother's clock. He stopped it at 12:55 p.m., immediately as mother passed from this life to the next. That was six years ago. It will never chime again.